Combination Cookery Book

2

Dear Sharp Customer,

We sincerely hope that you will enjoy your new Sharp Jet Convection/Microwave oven, and the new exciting world of microwave and dual cooking.

This cook book is designed to help you explore the many benefits of microwave and dual cooking, making meal preparation both easier and more convenient than ever before possible.

Please read both your cook book and instruction booklet carefully and thoroughly. This will make the use of your oven so much easier.

Recipes from all categories of food preparation — family favourites to gourmet recipes — are included, as well as basic information on microwave cooking and dual cooking. The versatility of your new Sharp Dual oven is apparent by just scanning the table of contents.

Use your Sharp Dual oven every time you prepare a meal. It will save you time and energy. As you become better acquainted with your new oven you will learn to easily convert your own favourite recipes to microwave or Dual cooking. As you become more au fait with your machine you will wonder how you managed before without a microwave.

If we can be of any further assistance do not hesitate to contact us. We are pleased that you chose a Sharp product, and hope you will enjoy using it.

Sincerely.

Sharp Home Economist
Sharp Microwave Oven Test Kitchen.

CONTENTS

RECIPES

DEFROSTING CHART FOR MEAT

FOOD	DEFROSTING TIME	VARIABLE CONTROL	METHOD	STANDING TIME
Joint (Beef, Pork, Lamb)	20-22 minutes/450g (1 lb)	LOW	Turn over after half the time. Shield as needed.	30-45 minutes
Minced Beef	7-8 minutes/450g (1 lb)	MED LOW	Break apart, remove any defrosted pieces as soon as possible. Place remainder in baking dish and continue to defrost.	15-30 minutes
Steak 1.87cm (¾") Thick	8-10 minutes/450g (1 lb)	MED LOW	Turn over after half the time. Shield as needed.	5-10 minutes
Chops	8-10 minutes/450g (1 lb)	MED LOW	Separate and turn over once. Shield as needed.	5-10 minutes
Liver	7-8 minutes/450g (1 lb)	MED LOW	Separate and re-arrange once. Shield as needed.	5-10 minutes
Sausages	7-8 minutes/450g (1 lb)	MED LOW	Separate and re-arrange once.	10 minutes
Bacon	5-7 minutes/450g (1 lb)	MED LOW	Separate rashers during defrosting.	5 minutes
Beefburgers	5-6 minutes/¼ pounder 4	MED LOW	Turn over after half defrosting time.	5-10 minutes
Veal Escallopes	6-8 minutes/450g (1 lb)	MED LOW	Turn over after half defrosting time. Shield as needed.	10-15 minutes

DEFROSTING CHART FOR POULTRY

FOOD	DEFROSTING TIME PER 450g (lb)	VARIABLE CONTROL	METHOD	STANDING TIME
Whole Chicken	18-20 minutes	LOW	Breast side down first. Turn over after third the time. Shield as needed.	30-45 minutes
Turkey	18-20 minutes	LOW	Breast side down first. Turn over after third the time. Shield as needed.	45-60 minutes
Duck	19-21 minutes	LOW	Breast side down first. Turn over after third the time. Shield as needed.	30-45 minutes
Pheasant	18-20 minutes	LOW	Breast side down first. Turn over after third the time. Shield as needed.	20-30 minutes
Chicken Drumsticks	7-8 minutes	MED LOW	Turn over after halfway through defrosting. Shield as needed.	10-15 minutes
Chicken Portions (Bone In)	7-8 minutes	MED LOW	Turn over after halfway through defrosting. Shield as needed.	10-15 minutes
Chicken Breasts (Boneless)	6-7 minutes	MED LOW	Turn over after halfway through defrosting. Shield as needed.	10-15 minutes
Rabbit	18-20 minutes	LOW	Turn over after halfway through defrosting. Shield as needed.	10-15 minutes

NOTE: For best results turn the joint of meat or poultry 2-3 times during defrosting.

DEFROSTING CHART FOR FISH

FOOD	DEFROSTING TIME	VARIABLE CONTROL	METHOD	STANDING TIME
Whole Fish (Trout/Mackerel)	5-8 minutes/450g (1 lb)	MED LOW	Do not layer fish, turn over halfway through defrosting. Shield as needed.	5-10 minutes
Fish Fillets	4-6 minutes/450g (1 lb)	MED LOW	Do not layer fish, turn over halfway through defrosting. Shield as needed.	5-10 minutes
Prawns	3-5 minutes/450g (1 lb)	MED LOW	Stir halfway through the defrosting.	10-12 minutes
Fish in Sauce (Boil in Bag)	3-5 minutes/175g (6oz)	MED LOW	Pierce bag. Place on plate. Turn over halfway through.	5 minutes

DEFROSTING CHART FOR FRUIT

FOOD	DEFROSTING TIME PER 450g (1 lb)	VARIABLE CONTROL	METHOD	STANDING TIME
Raspberries	5-7 minutes	MED LOW	Stir halfway through defrosting.	10 minutes
Apples	6-8 minutes	MED LOW	Stir halfway through defrosting.	10 minutes
Blackberries	5-7 minutes	MED LOW	Stir halfway through defrosting.	10 minutes
Gooseberries	5-7 minutes	MED LOW	Stir halfway through defrosting.	10 minutes
Rhubarb	4-6 minutes	MED LOW	Stir halfway through defrosting.	10 minutes
Blackcurrants	4-6 minutes	MED LOW	Stir halfway through defrosting.	10 minutes

GENERAL PROCEDURE
Place food on low metal rack on turntable.
Turn the food over once during defrosting.
Shield as needed, or directed by the chart.
After cooking leave for appropriate standing time.

MEAT COOKING CHART

MEAT COOKING CHART BY DUAL COOKING

FOOD		COOKING TIME PER 450g (1 lb)	SETTING MICROWAVE POWER/ TEMPERATURE
Beef Topside/ Silverside	Rare	9-11 minutes	MED 180°C
	Medium	11-13 minutes	MED 180°C
	Well done	14-16 minutes	MED 180°C
Rib of Beef	Rare	8-10 minutes	MED 180°C
	Medium	11-13 minutes	MED 180°C
	Well done	14-16 minutes	MED 180°C
Lamb leg	Medium	12-13 minutes	MED 180°C
	Well done	15-16 minutes	MED 180°C
Lamb fillet	Medium	12-13 minutes	MED 180°C
	Well done	15-16 minutes	MED 180°C
Lamb shoulder	Medium	11-13 minutes	MED 180°C
	Well done	14-16 minutes	MED 180°C
Pork leg/ loin/shoulder		15-17 minutes	MED 180°C

	STAGE	COOKING TIME PER 450g (1 lb)	MICROWAVE POWER	UTENSIL
Gammon	1	8-9 minutes +	HIGH	Low metal
	2	8-9 minutes	MED HIGH	Rack
Brisket Total cook time 2-4 lb weight	1	10 minutes +	HIGH	Low metal
	2	55-65 minutes	MED HIGH	Rack

MICROWAVE
1. For the gammon two stage cooking is required.
2. Brisket, should be placed in a heat proof (non-metallic) casserole dish. Covered with 2 pints of stock (and required amount of vegetables).
3. Turn joints of meat over 2-3 times during cooking time.
4. Allow to stand for 5-10 minutes.
5. When cooking meat by microwave place food on low metal rack.

DUAL COOK
1. Turn over 2-3 times during cooking
2. After cooking stand for 5-10 minutes.

COOKING CHART FOR SMALL CUTS OF MEAT BY MICROWAVE

FOOD	COOKING TIME PER 450g (lb)	MICROWAVE POWER	UTENSIL
Bacon	11-13 minutes	HIGH	Low metal Rack
Beefburgers (each 40-50g)	10-12 minutes	HIGH	Low metal Rack
Beefburgers (each 100g)	11-13 minutes	HIGH	Low metal Rack
Gammon Steaks	11-13 minutes	HIGH	Low metal Rack
Lamb Chops	9-10 minutes	HIGH	Low metal Rack
Pork Chops	10-11 minutes	HIGH	Low metal Rack
Sausages-thin	10-12 minutes	HIGH	Low metal Rack
Sausages-thick	11-13 minutes	HIGH	Low metal Rack
Beef Steak-Rare	See Grill Cooking Chart (Below)		
Beef Steak-Med	"	"	"
Beef Steak-Well Done	"	"	"

MICROWAVE
1. Turn food over halfway through cooking.
2. Place small items of food on a non-metallic heat proof dish, on the low metal rack.
3. Allow to stand for 1-2 minutes.

COOKING CHART FOR SMALL CUTS OF MEAT BY GRILL

FOOD	COOKING TIME	UTENSIL
Bacon	7-9 minutes	High metal Rack
Beefburgers (30-50g each)	6-8 minutes	High metal Rack
Beefburgers (100g each)	11-13 minutes	High metal Rack
Gammon Steaks	9-11 minutes	High metal Rack
Lamb Chops	19-22 minutes	High metal Rack
Pork Chops	19-22 minutes	High metal Rack
Sausages-thin	8-10 minutes	High metal Rack
Sausages-thick	8-11 minutes	High metal Rack
Beef Steak-Rare	5-7 minutes	High metal Rack
Beef Steak-Med	7-9 minutes	High metal Rack
Beef Steak-Well Done	11-13 minutes	High metal Rack

GRILL
1. Place item of food on a metal tray or heat proof dish on the metal rack.
2. Use of the high metal rack or low metal rack is a suggestion. It depends on personal preference as to how brown you like your food.
3. Turn item of food over 2-3 times during cooking.
4. Cooking times in the charts are a guide only they may vary depending on the initial temperature of the food and the temperature of the grill.
5. The above cooking times are for use with a cold grill.
6. Allow to stand for 1-2 minutes.

COOKING CHART FOR SMALL CUTS OF MEAT BY DUAL GRILL

FOOD	QUANTITY	APPROX. TOTAL WEIGHT	COOKING TIME (QUANTITY)	SMALL CUTS OF MEAT BY DUAL GRILL MICROWAVE POWER	UTENSIL
Bacon	2	100g	6-7 minutes	MED LOW	High metal Rack
Bacon	4	200g	8-9 minutes	MED LOW	High metal Rack
Bacon	6	400g	9-10 minutes	MED LOW	High metal Rack
Beefburgers	2	75-100g	4-6 minutes	MED LOW	High metal Rack
Beefburgers	4	150-200g	8-10 minutes	MED LOW	High metal Rack
Beefburgers	2	200g	8-10 minutes	MED LOW	High metal Rack
Beefburgers	4	400g	10-11 minutes	MED LOW	High metal Rack
Gammon Steaks	2	231g	7-10 minutes	MED LOW	High metal Rack
Gammon Steaks	4	396g	9-12 minutes	MED LOW	High metal Rack
Lamb Chops	2	148g	8-10 minutes	MED LOW	High metal Rack
Lamb Chops	4	520g	16-18 minutes	MED LOW	High metal Rack
Pork Chops	2	427g	8-10 minutes	MED LOW	High metal Rack
Pork Chops	4	822g	17-20 minutes	MED LOW	High metal Rack
Sausages-thin	2	32g	5-6 minutes	MED LOW	High metal Rack
Sausages-thin	4	64g	6-8 minutes	MED LOW	High metal Rack
Sausages-thin	6	96g	8-10 minutes	MED LOW	Low metal Rack
Sausages-thick	2	60g	6-8 minutes	MED LOW	High metal Rack
Sausages-thick	4	120g	10-13 minutes	MED LOW	Low metal Rack
Sausages-thick	6	180g	12-15 minutes	MED LOW	Low metal Rack
Beef Steak-Rare	2	400g	See Grill Cooking Chart (Page 10)		
Beef Steak-Med	2	400g	"	"	"
Beef Steak-Well Done	2	400g	"	"	"

DUAL GRILL
1. Place item of food on a metal tray or heat proof dish on the metal rack.
2. Use of the high metal rack or low metal rack is a suggestion. It depends on personal preference as to how brown you like your food.
3. Turn item of food over 2-3 times during cooking.
4. Cooking times in the charts are a guide only they may vary depending on the initial temperature of the food and the temperature of the grill.
5. The above cooking times are for use with a cold grill.
6. Allow to stand for 1-2 minutes.

POULTRY AND GAME COOKING CHARTS

POULTRY AND GAME COOKING CHART BY MICROWAVE				POULTRY AND GAME COOKING CHART BY DUAL COOK		
FOOD	COOKING TIME PER 450g (lb)	MICROWAVE POWER	UTENSIL	COOKING TIME PER 450g (lb)	SETTING MICROWAVE POWER/ TEMPERATURE	UTENSIL
Chicken -unstuffed	9-10 minutes	HIGH	Low metal Rack	8-9 minutes	MED 200°C	Low metal Rack
Turkey -unstuffed	9-10 minutes	HIGH	Low metal Rack	9-10 minutes	MED 180°C	Low metal Rack
Duck -unstuffed	9-10 minutes	HIGH	Low metal Rack	10-11 minutes	MED 180°C	Low metal Rack
Pheasant -unstuffed	8-9 minutes	HIGH	Low metal Rack	9-10 minutes	MED 180°C	Low metal Rack
Rabbit	8-9 minutes	HIGH	Low metal Rack	9-10 minutes	MED 180°C	Low metal Rack
Chicken portions	9-10 minutes	HIGH	Low metal Rack	9-10 minutes	MED 180°C	Low metal Rack
Chicken fillets	9-10 minutes	HIGH	Low metal Rack	—	—	—
Duck portions	9-10 minutes	HIGH	Low metal Rack	9-10 minutes	MED 180°C	Low metal Rack
Rabbit portions	8-9 minutes	HIGH	Low metal Rack	—	—	—

MICROWAVE
1. Turn poultry over 2-3 times during cooking.
2. After cooking stand for 5-10 minutes.

DUAL COOK
1. Turn poultry over 2-3 times during cooking.
2. After cooking stand for 5-10 minutes.

FISH COOKING CHARTS BY MICROWAVE

| | FISH COOKING CHART BY MICROWAVE | | | FROZEN FISH COOKING CHART BY MICROWAVE | | |
FOOD	COOKING TIME PER 450g (lb)	MICROWAVE POWER	METHOD	COOKING TIME PER 450g (lb)	MICROWAVE POWER	METHOD
Cod steaks	5-10 minutes	HIGH	Place in non-metallic dish. Cover.	—	—	—
Haddock fillets	4-5 minutes	HIGH	Place in non-metallic dish. Cover.	10-12 minutes	HIGH	Place in non-metallic dish. Cover.
Hoki fillets	4-5 minutes	HIGH	Place in non-metallic dish. Cover.	—	—	—
Plaice fillets	4-5 minutes	HIGH	Place in non-metallic dish. Cover.	10-12 minutes	HIGH	Place in non-metallic dish. Cover.
Salmon -whole	7-8 minutes	MED HIGH	Place in non-metallic dish. Cover.	—	—	—
Trout-whole	5-6 minutes	HIGH	Place in non-metallic dish. Cover.	10-12 minutes	HIGH	Place in non-metallic dish. Cover.
Lemon Sole Dover Sole	4-6 minutes	HIGH	Turn over halfway through cooking	—	—	—

MICROWAVE
1. Place in thin layer.
2. Allow to stand for 2-3 minutes.

FISH COOKING CHARTS BY GRILL AND DUAL GRILL

| | FISH COOKING CHART BY MICROWAVE AND GRILL | | | FISH COOKING CHART BY GRILL | |
FOOD	COOKING TIME PER 450g (lb)	MICROWAVE POWER	METHOD	COOKING TIME PER 450g (lb)	METHOD
Cod steaks	8-9 minutes	MED	Low metal Rack	—	—
Haddock fillets	8-9 minutes	MED	Low metal Rack	—	—
Hoki fillets	8-9 minutes	MED	Low metal Rack	11-12 minutes	Low metal Rack
Plaice fillets	8-9 minutes	MED	Low metal Rack	11-12 minutes	Low metal Rack
Trout -whole	9-10 minutes	MED	High metal Rack	14-16 minutes	Low metal Rack

GRILL AND DUAL GRILL
1. Place in thin layer.
2. Turn over halfway through cooking time.
3. When cooking certain types of fish it may be necessary to place on a metal tray or heatproof dish.
4. Allow to stand for 2-3 minutes.

FROZEN VEGETABLE COOKING CHARTS

VEGETABLE	QUANTITY	WATER	METHOD	MINUTES ON HIGH
Asparagus	450g/1 lb	2 x 15ml (2 tbsp)	Use 1 litre (1¾ pt) casserole dish	5-6 minutes
Beans, broad	450g/1 lb	2 x 15ml (2 tbsp)	Use 1 litre (1¾ pt) casserole dish	8-9 minutes
Beans, whole green	450g/1 lb	2 x 15ml (2 tbsp)	Use 1 litre (1¾ pt) casserole dish	9-11 minutes
Broccoli, spears	450g/1 lb	2 x 15ml (2 tbsp)	Use 1 litre (1¾ pt) casserole dish	9-11 minutes
Brussels sprouts	450g/1 lb	2 x 15ml (2 tbsp)	Use 1 litre (1¾ pt) casserole dish	9-11 minutes
Cabbage, shredded	450g/1 lb	2 x 15ml (2 tbsp)	Use 1½ litre (3 pt) casserole dish	8-9 minutes
Carrots, sliced	450g/1 lb	2 x 15ml (2 tbsp)	Use 1 litre (1¾ pt) casserole dish	8-9 minutes
Carrots, whole	450g/1 lb	2 x 15ml (2 tbsp)	Use 1½ litre (3 pt) casserole dish	8-9 minutes
Cauliflower, florets	450g/1 lb	2 x 15ml (2 tbsp)	Use 1 litre (1¾ pt) casserole dish	8-9 minutes
Courgettes, sliced	450g/1 lb	2 x 15ml (2 tbsp)	Use 1 litre (1¾ pt) casserole dish	8-9 minutes
Corn, baby	450g/1 lb	2 x 15ml (2 tbsp)	Use 1½ litre (3 pt) casserole dish	9-10 minutes
Corn on the cob	1 cob 2 cobs		Place in dish and cover Place in dish and cover	5-7 minutes 6-8 minutes
Leeks, sliced	225g/8 oz	2 x 15ml (2 tbsp)	Place in dish	5-6 minutes
Mange tout	450g/1 lb	2 x 15ml (2 tbsp)	Place in a dish	9-10 minutes
Mixed vegetables	450g/1 lb	2 x 15ml (2 tbsp)	Place in dish and cover	8-10 minutes
Mushrooms, whole	450g/1 lb	2 x 15ml (2 tbsp)	Place in dish	7 minutes
Parsnip, whole	450g/1 lb	2 x 15ml (2 tbsp)	Place in dish	9-10 minutes
Peas	225g/8 oz	2 x 15ml (2 tbsp)	Place in dish	5-6 minutes
Ratatouille	450g/1 lb	2 x 15ml (2 tbsp)	Place in dish	8-9 minutes
Spinach leaf, chopped	450g/1 lb	2 x 15ml (2 tbsp)	Place in dish	9-11 minutes
Swede, diced	450g/1 lb	2 x 15ml (2 tbsp)	Use 1 litre (1¾ pt) casserole dish	9-10 minutes

All vegetables should be cooked in a covered dish.
All vegetables should be stirred half way through cooking.
Allow cooked vegetables to stand for 2-3 minutes.

FRESH VEGETABLE COOKING CHARTS

VEGETABLE	QUANTITY	WATER	METHOD	MINUTES ON HIGH
Globe artichokes	2 medium	6 x 15ml (6 tbsp)	Rinse with water.	6-7 minutes
Asparagus spears	450g/1 lb	6 x 15ml (6 tbsp)	Rinse with water.	6-7 minutes
Aubergine	450g/1 lb	2 x 15ml (2 tbsp)	Slice the aubergine.	6-7 minutes
Beans-French	450g/1 lb	4 x 15ml (4 tbsp)	Trim. Rinse with water.	4-5 minutes
Beetroot	4 medium		Cover with water.	16-19 minutes
Broccoli	450g/1 lb	3 x 15ml (3 tbsp)	Remove tough part of stalk.	4-5 minutes
Brussels Sprouts	450g/1 lb	3 x 15ml (3 tbsp)	Trim. Rinse with water.	7-8 minutes
Cabbage	450g/1 lb	2 x 15ml (2 tbsp)	Wash, and chop.	6 minutes
Celery	450g/1 lb	6 x 15ml (6 tbsp)	Trim. Rinse with water slice in half.	7 minutes
Carrots	450g/1 lb	3 x 15ml (3 tbsp)	Peel and slice.	7-8 minutes
Cauliflower	450g/1 lb	3 x 15ml (3 tbsp)	Cut into florets.	9-10 minutes
Corn on the cob	2 cobs 4 cobs 6 cobs	5 x 15ml (5 tbsp)	Peel back husks. Remove silk.	3-5 minutes 7-9 minutes 11-13 minutes
Courgettes	450g/1 lb	2 x 15ml (2 tbsp)	Sliced.	6 minutes
Leeks	450g/1 lb	2 x 15ml (2 tbsp)	Sliced.	5-6 minutes
Mushrooms	450g/1 lb	2 x 15ml (2 tbsp)	Rinse.	3 minutes
Onions	450g/1 lb	2 x 15ml (2 tbsp)	Peel and slice.	5 minutes
Parsnips, diced quartered	450g/1 lb	4 x 15ml (4 tbsp)	Rinse and prepare.	8 minutes 8 minutes
Peas	450g/1 lb	2 x 15ml (2 tbsp)	Shell.	4-5 minutes
Potatoes Baked	2 medium 4 medium		Pierce skin, wrap in paper towel.	9-10 minutes 14-16 minutes
Boiled	450g/1 lb	2 x 15ml (2 tbsp)	Peel. Cut into quarters.	5-7 minutes
New	450g/1 lb	2 x 15ml (2 tbsp)	Scrape.	6-7 minutes
Spinach	450g/1 lb	1 x 15ml (1 tbsp)	Wash.	7 minutes
Spring Greens	450g/1 lb	1 x 15ml (1 tbsp)	Wash. Remove thick stem.	5-6 minutes
Swede	450g/1 lb	2 x 15ml (2 tbsp)	Peel and dice.	4-6 minutes
Tomatoes	450g/1 lb		Clean, peel halve.	6 minutes
Turnips	450g/1 lb	4 x 15ml (4 tbsp)	Wash, peel, dice.	7 minutes

All vegetables should be cooked in a covered dish.
Allow cooked vegetables to stand for 2-3 minutes.

RICE AND PASTA COOKING CHART

ITEM	WEIGHT Kg/g	QUANTITY WATER	STARTING TEMPERATURE WATER	POWER LEVEL	COOK TIME	STANDING TIME
Long grain rice	225g/8oz	600ml (1pt)	60°C	HIGH	9-10 minutes	10 minutes
Brown rice	225g/8oz	600ml (1pt)	60°C	HIGH	10-13 minutes	10 minutes
Spaghetti	225g/8oz	900ml (1½pt)	60°C	HIGH	9-10 minutes	10 minutes
Maccaroni	225g/8oz	900ml (1½pt)	60°C	HIGH	8-9 minutes	10 minutes
Tagliatelle	225g/8oz	900ml (1½pt)	60°C	HIGH	6-8 minutes	10 minutes
Pasta shells	225g/8oz	900ml (1½pt)	60°C	HIGH	9-10 minutes	10-12 minutes
Fresh tagliatelle	267g	Cover with water.	100°C	HIGH	4-5 minutes	15 minutes
Fresh taglionni	265g	Cover with water.	100°C	HIGH	3-4 minutes	10 minutes
Fresh cappeletti	255g	Cover with water.	100°C	HIGH	4-5 minutes	10 minutes
Fresh ravioli	265g	Cover with water.	100°C	HIGH	5-6 minutes	10 minutes

1. Cook pasta in a large non-metallic casserole dish.
2. Cover with microwave plastic wrap.
3. Stir after cooking.

GRILLING CHARTS

FOOD	QUANTITY	1ST STAGE	METHOD	2ND STAGE	UTENSIL	NOTES
Toast -medium sliced	2 slices	4 minutes	Turn over	1-2 minutes	High metal Rack	
Toast fresh cut	2 slices	4 minutes	Turn over	1-2 minutes	High metal Rack	
Toasted cheese sandwich	1	4 minutes	Turn over	2 minutes	High metal Rack	Make up cheese sandwich and then toast.
Cheese on toast	2 slices	4 minutes	Turn over	3 minutes	High metal Rack	After 1st stage place cheese on toast.
Bread roll -halved	1	3 minutes	Turn over	2 minutes	High metal Rack	
Tea cake -halved	1	3 minutes	Turn over	1½ minutes	High metal Rack	
Crumpets	2	2 minutes	Turn over	2 minutes	High metal Rack	
Gratin -just to brown		7 minutes			High metal Rack	

MISCELLANEOUS FOOD CHART

FOOD	INGREDIENTS	METHOD	VARIABLE CONTROL	COOKING TIME
Scrambled eggs		Melt Butter for ½ min. on HIGH. Beat eggs and milk together. Add to butter. Stir half-way through cooking time.		
1 x size 3	1 tbsp (15ml) milk ½ tbsp (½ oz) butter		HIGH	1-1½ minutes
2 x size 3	2 tbsp (30ml) milk ½ tbsp (½ oz) butter		HIGH	1½ minutes
4 x size 3	2 tbsp (30ml) milk ½ tbsp (½ oz) butter		HIGH	2-2½ minutes
6 x size 3	4 tbsp (60ml) milk 1 tbsp (1 oz) butter		HIGH	3½ minutes
Baked eggs	2 x size 3 eggs	Place eggs in two glass/ceramic dishes. Pierce yolks carefully. Leave uncovered.	MED HIGH	1½ minutes
Poached eggs	2 x size 3 eggs 1 tbsp water per ramekin/glass dish.	Place 1 tbsp water in each dish with egg. Pierce yolk.	MED HIGH	1½ minutes
Melting jelly	1 x packet jelly 2 tbsp (30ml) water	Place jelly and water in microwavable bowl.	HIGH	1 minute
Defrosting shortcrust pastry	13 oz pastry	Leave to stand after defrosting.	MED LOW	2 minutes
Defrosting puff pastry	13 oz pastry	Leave to stand after defrosting.	MED LOW	3 minutes
Toasted almonds	25g (1 oz) flaked almonds. Knob of butter	Place almonds in dish with butter.	HIGH	2-3 minutes
Porridge	2 tbsp (30ml) oats ¼ pt. milk	Place oats in cereal bowl. Mix in milk.	HIGH	2 minutes
Custard	1 tbsp (15ml) custard powder 1 tbsp sugar ½ pt. milk	Mix all the ingredients in bowl.	HIGH	3 minutes
Plated meal (At room temp.)			MED HIGH	6 minutes
Melting chocolate	125g chocolate	Break up and place in bowl. Stir after 1 minute.	HIGH	1 minute
Drinking chocolate	3 tbsp (45ml) chocolate, 1 cup milk	Place chocolate and milk in jug. Stir well after cooking.	HIGH	1½-2 minutes
Baked potatoes	4 medium potatoes	Pierce potatoes with fork several times. Place on turntable.	DUAL COOK MICROWAVE-MED CONVECTION-200°C	15 minutes
Juice from orange/lemon	1 orange/lemon	Slice fruit in half. Place on edge of turntable.	HIGH	30 seconds-1 minute

COOKING CHART FOR FROZEN CONVENIENCE FOOD BY MICROWAVE

FOOD	QUANTITY	APPROX. WEIGHT	COOKING TIME	MICROWAVE POWER	UTENSIL
Bernard Mathews					
Turkey roast	1	580g	50-55 minutes	MED	Low metal Rack
Lamb roast	1	580g	40-45 minutes	MED	Low metal Rack
Meat dishes					
Beefburgers	2	110g	4-4½ minutes	HIGH	Low metal Rack
Beefburgers	4	230g	5½-6 minutes	HIGH	Low metal Rack
Beefburgers	2	210g	6-7 minutes	HIGH	Low metal Rack
Beefburgers	4	430g	9-10 minutes	HIGH	Low metal Rack
Steaklet grills	2	170g	4-4½ minutes	HIGH	Low metal Rack
Steaklet grills	4	340g	6-6½ minutes	HIGH	Low metal Rack
Faggots in gravy	4	390g	11-13 minutes	MED HIGH	Low metal Rack
Minced beef in gravy	1	170g	6-7 minutes	HIGH	Low metal Rack
Lean beef in gravy	1	225g	8-9 minutes	HIGH	Low metal Rack
Shepherds pie	1	300g	See Dual Cook/Dual Grill Charts (Pages 21, 23)		
Chicken casserole	1	170g	6-7 minutes	HIGH	Low metal Rack
Mousaka	1	300g	See Dual Cook Chart (Page 21)		—
Cannelloni	1	340g	See Dual Cook/Dual Grill Charts (Pages 21, 23)		
Plated meal (Birds Eye)	1	340g	10-12 minutes	HIGH	Low metal Rack
Uncooked pies					
Steak and kidney-small	1	145g	See Dual Cook Chart (Page 21)		
Steak and kidney-large	1	450g	"	"	"
Chicken pie -small	1	160g	"	"	"
Chicken pie -large	1	450g	"	"	"
Pre-cooked					
Meat pies-small	1	230g	"	"	"
Meat pies-large	1	610g	"	"	"
Cornish pastie	1	110g	1½-2 minutes	HIGH	Low metal Rack
Cornish pastie	2		3½-4 minutes	HIGH	Low metal Rack
Sausage rolls	1	60g	1½-2 minutes	HIGH	Low metal Rack
Sausage rolls	2		3½-4 minutes	HIGH	Low metal Rack

COOKING CHART FOR FROZEN
CONVENIENCE FOOD BY MICROWAVE (CONT.)

FOOD	QUANTITY	APPROX. WEIGHT	COOKING TIME	MICROWAVE POWER	UTENSIL
Part-cooked-chicken					
Chicken kiev	2	280g	See Dual Grill Cooking Chart (Page 24)		
Mini kievs	12	270g	See Dual Cook/Dual Grill Charts (Pages 22, 24)		
Chicken drumsticks	4	135g	13-16 minutes	MED HIGH	Low metal Rack
Chicken drummers	6	340g	11-13 minutes	MED HIGH	Low metal Rack
Chicken nuggets	30	425g	See Dual Cook/Dual Grill Charts (Page 22, 24)		
Turkey burgers	4	235g	7-9 minutes	MED HIGH	Low metal Rack
Chicken + cheeseburgers	4	235g	7-9 minutes	MED HIGH	Low metal Rack
Fish					
Boil in the bags kipper fillets	1	170g	5-6 minutes	MED HIGH	Low metal Rack
Fish cakes	4	210g	7-9 minutes	MED HIGH	Low metal Rack
Fish fingers	4	110g	3-4 minutes	MED HIGH	Low metal Rack
Fish fingers	6	170g	4-5 minutes	MED HIGH	Low metal Rack
Fishermans pie	1	340g	17-19 minutes	MED	Low metal Rack
Haddock fillets in bread crumbs	2	225g	9-11 minutes	MED HIGH	Low metal Rack
Pizza 5''	1	110g	2½-3 minutes	HIGH	Low metal Rack
Pizza 8-10'' thick	1	500g	6-7 minutes	MED HIGH	Low metal Rack
Pizza slice	1	140g	See Dual Cook/Dual Grill Charts (Pages 22, 24)		
French bread pizza	1	135g	"	"	"
Garlic pizza bread	1	200g	"	"	"
Part cooked garlic bread	1	200g	See Dual Cook Chart (Page 22)		
Quiche	1	340g	9-11 minutes	MED HIGH	Low metal Rack
Potatoes + Vegetables					
Jacket potatoes	2	450g	See Dual Cook/Dual Grill Charts (Page 22, 24)		
Oven crunches	—	300g	"	"	"
Potato waffles	4	240g	See Dual Grill Cooking Chart (Page 24)		
Jacket scallops	—	300g	See Dual Cook/Dual Grill Charts (Page 22, 24)		
Stir fry rice	1	340g	8-9 minutes	MED HIGH	Low metal Rack
Oven chips	—	450g	See Dual Cook/Dual Grill Charts (Page 22, 24)		
Desserts					
Apple pie	1	460g	18-20 minutes	MED HIGH	Low metal Rack
Apple danish bar	1	400g	15-20 minutes	MED HIGH	Low metal Rack
Spotted dick	1	350g	3-4 minutes	MED HIGH	Low metal Rack

MICROWAVE
1. Remove from foil container.
2. Place small items on a non-metallic heat proof dish on low metal rack.
3. Allow to stand for 2-3 minutes.
4. Bernard Mathews Roasts; turn over half way through cooking and allow to stand for 15-20 minutes, wrapped in foil, at end of cooking time.
5. Stir half way through cooking were possible.

COOKING CHART FOR FROZEN CONVENIENCE FOOD BY DUAL COOK

FOOD	QUANTITY	APPROX. WEIGHT	COOKING TIME	MICROWAVE POWER	CON-VECTION	UTENSIL
Bernard Mathews						
Turkey roast	1	580g	50-55 minutes	MED LOW	200°C	Low metal Rack
Lamb roast	1	580g	45-50 minutes	MED LOW	200°C	Low metal Rack
Meat dishes						
Beefburgers	2	110g	See Microwave and Dual Grill Charts (Page 19, 23)			
Beefburgers	4	230g	"	"	"	"
Beefburgers	2	210g	"	"	"	"
Beefburgers	4	430g	"	"	"	"
Steaklet grills	2	170g	"	"	"	"
Steaklet grills	4	340g	"	"	"	"
Faggots in gravy	4	390g	See Microwave Cooking Chart (Page 19)			
Minced beef in gravy	1	170g	"	"	"	"
Lean beef in gravy	1	225g	"	"	"	"
Shepherds pie	1	300g	9-10 minutes	MED HIGH	200°C	Low metal Rack
Chicken casserole	1	170g	See Microwave Cooking Chart (Page 19)			
Mousaka	1	300g	17-19 minutes	MED HIGH	200°C	Low metal Rack
Cannelloni	1	340g	11-14 minutes	MED HIGH	200°C	Low metal Rack
Plated meal (Birds Eye)	1	340g	See Microwave Cooking Chart (Page 19)			
Uncooked pies						
Steak and kidney-small	1	145g	13-15 minutes	MED LOW	200°C	Low metal Rack
Steak and kidney-large	1	450g	20-22 minutes	MED LOW	200°C	Low metal Rack
Chicken pie -small	1	160g	15-18 minutes	MED LOW	200°C	Low metal Rack
Chicken pie -large	1	450g	20-22 minutes	MED LOW	200°C	Low metal Rack
Pre-cooked						
Meat pies-small	1	230g	8-10 minutes	MED	200°C	Low metal Rack
Meat pies-large	1	610g	14-16 minutes	MED	200°C	Low metal Rack
Cornish pastie	1	110g	6-7 minutes	MED	200°C	Low metal Rack
Cornish pastie	2		8-10 minutes	MED	200°C	Low metal Rack
Sausage rolls	1	60g	1½-2 minutes	MED	200°C	Low metal Rack
Sausage rolls	2		2-3 minutes	MED	200°C	Low metal Rack

FOOD	QUANTITY	APPROX. WEIGHT	COOKING TIME	SETTING MICROWAVE POWER/ TEMPERATURE	UTENSIL
Part-cooked-chicken					
Chicken kiev	2	280g	See Dual Grill Cooking Chart (Page 24)		
Mini kievs	12	270g	10-12 minutes	MED LOW 200°C	Low metal Rack
Chicken drumsticks	4	135g	See Microwave Cooking Chart (Page 20)		
Chicken drummers	6	340g	13-15 minutes	MED 200°C	Low metal Rack
Chicken nuggets	30	425g	12-13 minutes	MED 200°C	Low metal Rack
Turkey burgers	4	235g	13-15 minutes	MED 200°C	Low metal Rack
Chicken + cheese burgers	4	235g	13-15 minutes	MED 200°C	Low metal Rack
Fish					
Boil in the bags kipper fillets	1	170g	See Microwave Cooking Chart (Page 20)		
Fish cakes	4	210g	See Microwave and Dual Grill Charts (Page 20, 24)		
Fish fingers	4	110g	"	"	"
Fish fingers	6	170g	"	"	"
Fishermans pie	1	340g	18-20 minutes	MED 200°C	Low metal Rack
Haddock fillets in bread crumbs	2	225g	13-15 minutes	MED 200°C	Low metal Rack
Pizza 5''	1	110g	5-6 minutes	MED LOW 200°C	Low metal Rack
Pizza 8-10'' thick	1	500g	16-18 minutes	MED LOW 200°C	Low metal Rack
Pizza slice	1	140g	7-8 minutes	MED LOW 200°C	Low metal Rack
French bread pizza	1	135g	6-7 minutes	MED LOW 200°C	Low metal Rack
Garlic pizza bread	1	200g	5-6 minutes	MED LOW 200°C	Low metal Rack
Part cooked garlic bread	1	200g	8-9 minutes	LOW 200°C	—
Quiche	1	340g	18-20 minutes	MED LOW 200°C	—
Potatoes + Vegetables					
Jacket potatoes	2	450g	13-15 minutes	MED 200°C	Low metal Rack
Oven crunchies	—	300g	11-12 minutes	MED 200°C	—
Potato waffles	4	240g	See Dual Grill Cooking Chart (Page 24)		
Jacket scallops	—	300g	11-12 minutes	MED LOW 200°C	—
Stir fry rice	1	340g	See Microwave Cooking Chart (Page 20)		
Oven chips	—	450g	14-15 minutes	MED 200°C	Low metal Rack
Desserts					
Apple pie	1	460g	18-20 minutes	MED LOW 200°C	Low metal Rack
Apple danish bar	1	400g	15-16 minutes	MED LOW 200°C	Low metal Rack
Spotted dick	1	350g	18-20 minutes	MED LOW 200°C	Low metal Rack

DUAL COOK

1. Place small items on metallic or heat proof dish on metal rack.
2. Turn items of food over if necessary.
3. Cooking times in the chart are a guide only they may vary depending on the initial temperature of the food and the temperature of the grill or oven.
4. Standing time 2-3 minutes.
5. Bernard Mathews Roasts; turn over half way through cooking and allow to stand for 15-20 minutes, wrapped in foil, at end of cooking time.

COOKING CHART FOR FROZEN CONVENIENCE FOOD BY DUAL GRILL

FOOD	QUANTITY	APPROX. WEIGHT	COOKING TIME	MICROWAVE POWER	UTENSIL
Bernard Mathews					
Turkey roast	1	580g	See Microwave/Dual Cook Charts (Pages 19, 21)		
Lamb roast	1	580g	"	"	"
Meat dishes					
Beefburgers	2	110g	4-5 minutes	MED	Low metal Rack
Beefburgers	4	230g	6-7 minutes	MED	Low metal Rack
Beefburgers	2	210g	8-9 minutes	MED	Low metal Rack
Beefburgers	4	430g	11-12 minutes	MED	Low metal Rack
Steaklet grills	2	170g	8-9 minutes	MED	Low metal Rack
Steaklet grills	4	340g	9-11 minutes	MED	Low metal Rack
Faggots in gravy	4	390g	See Microwave Cooking Chart (Page 19)		
Minced beef in gravy	1	170g	"	"	"
Lean beef in gravy	1	225g	"	"	"
Shepherds pie	1	300g	9-10 minutes	MED HIGH	Low metal Rack
Chicken casserole	1	170g	See Microwave Cooking Chart (Page 19)		
Mousaka	1	300g	See Dual Cook Charts (Page 21)		
Cannelloni	1	340g	12-13 minutes	MED HIGH	Low metal Rack
Plated meal (Birds Eye)	1	340g	See Microwave Cooking Chart (Page 19)		
Uncooked pies					
Steak and kidney-small	1	145g	See Dual Cook Chart (Page 21)		
Steak and kidney-large	1	450g	"	"	"
Chicken pie -small	1	160g	"	"	"
Chicken pie -large	1	450g	"	"	"
Pre-cooked					
Meat pies-small	1	230g	"	"	"
Meat pies-large	1	610g	"	"	"
Cornish pastie	1	110g	See Microwave/Dual Cook Charts (Pages 19, 21)		
Cornish pastie	2		"	"	"
Sausage rolls	1	60g	"	"	"
Sausage rolls	2		"	"	"

COOKING CHART FOR FROZEN
CONVENIENCE FOOD BY DUAL GRILL (CONT.)

FOOD	QUANTITY	APPROX. WEIGHT	COOKING TIME	MICROWAVE POWER	UTENSIL
Part-cooked-chicken					
Chicken kiev	2	280g	9-11 minutes	MED HIGH	Low metal Rack
Mini kievs	12	270g	8-10 minutes	MED LOW	High metal Rack
Chicken drumsticks	4	135g	See Microwave Cooking Chart (Page 20)		
Chicken drummers	6	340g	See Microwave/Dual Cook Charts (Pages 20, 22)		
Chicken nuggets	30	425g	9-10 minutes	MED	High metal Rack
Turkey burgers	4	235g	9-10 minutes	MED HIGH	High metal Rack
Chicken + cheeseburgers	4	235g	9-10 minutes	MED HIGH	High metal Rack
Fish					
Boil in the bags kipper fillets	1	170g	See Microwave Cooking Chart (Page 20)		
Fish cakes	4	210g	6-7 minutes	MED HIGH	High metal Rack
Fish fingers	4	110g	5-6 minutes	MED	High metal Rack
Fish fingers	6	170g	7-8 minutes	MED	High metal Rack
Fishermans pie	1	340g	See Microwave/Dual Cook Charts (Pages 20, 22)		
Haddock fillets in bread crumbs	2	225g	9-10 minutes	MED	High metal Rack
Pizza 5''	1	110g	5 minutes	MED LOW	High metal Rack
Pizza 8-10'' thick	1	500g	15-16 minutes	MED LOW	Low metal Rack
Pizza slice	1	140g	7-8 minutes	MED LOW	Low metal Rack
French bread pizza	1	135g	7 minutes	MED LOW	Low metal Rack
Garlic pizza bread	1	200g	7 minutes	MED LOW	Low metal Rack
Part cooked garlic bread	1	200g	See Dual Cook Chart (Page 22)		
Quiche	1	340g	See Microwave/Dual Cook Charts (Pages 20, 22)		
Potatoes + Vegetables					
Jacket potatoes	2	450g	11-12 minutes	MED	Low metal Rack
Oven crunches	—	300g	11-12 minutes	MED LOW	Low metal Rack
Potato waffles	4	240g	7 minutes	MED LOW	Low metal Rack
Jacket scallops	—	300g	11-12 minutes	MED LOW	Low metal Rack
Stir fry rice	1	340g	See Microwave Cooking Chart (Page 20)		
Oven chips	—	450g	15 minutes	MED HIGH	Low metal Rack
Desserts					
Apple pie	1	460g	See Microwave/Dual Cook Charts (Pages 20, 22)		
Apple danish bar	1	400g	"	"	"
Spotted dick	1	350g	"	"	"

DUAL GRILL
1. Place small items on metallic or heat proof dish on metal rack.
2. Turn items of food over if necessary.
3. Cooking times in the chart are a guide only they may vary depending on the initial temperature of the food and the temperature of the grill or oven.
4. Standing time 2-3 minutes.

REHEATING CHART BY MICROWAVE

ITEM	QUANTITY	APPROX. TOTAL WEIGHT	COOKING TIME	MICROWAVE POWER	UTENSILS
Meat pies (Individual)	1	140g	2-2½ minutes	HIGH	Low metal Rack
	2	280g	3-4 minutes	HIGH	Low metal Rack
Meat pies (Family)	1	445g	4-5 minutes	HIGH	Low metal Rack
Sausage rolls	1	65g	20-30 seconds	HIGH	Low metal Rack
Sausage rolls	2	130g	40-50 seconds	HIGH	Low metal Rack
Cornish pasties	1	120g	1 minute	HIGH	Low metal Rack
Cornish pasties	2	240g	1-1½ minutes	HIGH	Low metal Rack
Quiche (one slice)	1	110g	1-2 minutes	HIGH	Low metal Rack
Quiche	1	435g	4 minutes	HIGH	Low metal Rack
Pizza - small	1	120g	2-2½ minutes	HIGH	Low metal Rack
Pizza - large	1	545g	5-6 minutes	HIGH	Low metal Rack
Bread rolls	2	90g	See Dual Cook Reheating Chart (Page 26)		
Bread rolls	4	180g	"	"	"
Garlic bread	1	200g	"	"	"
Garlic pizza bread	1	200g	"	"	"
Croissants	1	40g	10-20 seconds	HIGH	Low metal Rack
Croissants	2	80g	20 seconds	HIGH	Low metal Rack
Onion bhajis	2	50g	1 minute	HIGH	Low metal Rack
Onion bhajis	4	110g	1½ minutes	HIGH	Low metal Rack
Samosas	4	200g	See Dual Cook/Dual Grill Reheating Charts (Pages 26, 27)		
Spring rolls	2	—	See Dual Cook Reheating Chart (Page 26)		
Spring rolls	4	—	"	"	"
Fruit pie Small	2	50g	20 seconds	HIGH	Low metal Rack
	4	100g	20-30 seconds	HIGH	Low metal Rack
Fruit pie Large	1	545g	1-1½ minutes	HIGH	Low metal Rack

MICROWAVE
1. Remove from foil containers.
2. For some items eg. small items place on a non-metallic dish on the low rack.
3. Allow to stand for 30 seconds-2 minutes depending on the item of food.

REHEATING CHART BY DUAL COOK

ITEM	QUANTITY	APPROX. TOTAL WEIGHT	COOKING TIME	MICROWAVE POWER	CONVECTION	UTENSIL
Meat pies (Individual)	1	140g	7-10 minutes	MED	200°C	Low metal Rack
	2	280g	10-12 minutes	MED	200°C	Low metal Rack
Meat pies (Family)	1	445g	11-12 minutes	MED	200°C	Low metal Rack
Sausage rolls	1	65g	6-7 minutes	LOW	200°C	Low metal Rack
Sausage rolls	2	130g	9-10 minutes	LOW	200°C	Low metal Rack
Cornish pasties	1	120g	6-7 minutes	MED LOW	200°C	Low metal Rack
Cornish pasties	2	240g	9-10 minutes	MED LOW	200°C	Low metal Rack
Quiche (one slice)	1	110g	See Microwave Reheating Chart (Page 25)			
Quiche	1	435g	10-13 minutes	MED LOW	200°C	Low metal Rack
Pizza - small	1	120g	4½-5½ minutes	MED LOW	200°C	Low metal Rack
Pizza - large	1	545g	11-12 minutes	MED LOW	200°C	Low metal Rack
Bread rolls	2	90g	3-5 minutes	LOW	200°C	Low metal Rack
Bread rolls	4	180g	5-7 minutes	LOW	200°C	Low metal Rack
Garlic bread	1	200g	7-10 minutes	LOW	200°C	Low metal Rack
Garlic pizza bread	1	200g	7-10 minutes	LOW	200°C	Low metal Rack
Croissants	1	40g	1 minute	LOW	200°C	Low metal Rack
Croissants	2	80g	1½-2 minutes	LOW	200°C	Low metal Rack
Onion bhajis	2	50g	5-7 minutes	LOW	200°C	Low metal Rack
Onion bhajis	4	110g	6-7 minutes	LOW	200°C	Low metal Rack
Samosas	4	200g	9-10 minutes	MED LOW	200°C	Low metal Rack
Spring rolls	2	—	8-9 minutes	MED LOW	200°C	Low metal Rack
Spring rolls	4	—	9-10 minutes	MED LOW	200°C	Low metal Rack
Fruit pie Small	2	50g	2-3 minutes	LOW	200°C	Low metal Rack
	4	100g	3-5 minutes	LOW	200°C	Low metal Rack
Fruit pie Large	1	545g	See Microwave Reheating Chart (Page 25)			

DUAL COOK AND DUAL GRILL
1. For small items it may be necessary to place them on a heatproof dish on the metal rack. This will also help prevent arcing in the oven.
2. Allow to stand for 30 seconds-2 minutes depending on the item of food.

The reheating times are a rough guide only as the initial temperature of the food will affect the required reheating times.

REHEATING CHART BY DUAL GRILL

ITEM	QUANTITY	APPROX. TOTAL WEIGHT	COOKING TIME	MICROWAVE POWER	UTENSIL
Meat pies (Individual)	1	140g	See Microwave/Dual Cook Reheating Charts (Pages 25, 26)		
	2	280g	"	"	"
Meat pies (Family)	1	445g	"	"	"
Sausage rolls	1	65g	3-4 minutes	LOW	Low metal Rack
Sausage rolls	2	130g	4-5 minutes	LOW	Low metal Rack
Cornish pasties	1	120g	4-5 minutes	LOW	Low metal Rack
Cornish pasties	2	240g	5-7 minutes	LOW	Low metal Rack
Quiche (one slice)	1	110g	See Microwave Reheating Chart (Page 25)		
Quiche	1	435g	10-13 minutes	MED LOW	Low metal Rack
Pizza - small	1	120g	$3\frac{1}{2}$-$4\frac{1}{2}$ minutes	MED LOW	Low metal Rack
Pizza - large	1	545g	6-7 minutes	MED LOW	Low metal Rack
Bread rolls	2	90g	See Dual Cook Reheating Chart (Page 26)		
Bread rolls	4	180g	"	"	"
Garlic bread	1	200g	"	"	"
Garlic pizza bread	1	200g	8-10 minutes	LOW	Low metal Rack
Croissants	1	40g	See Microwave/Dual Cook Reheating Charts (Pages 25, 26)		
Croissants	2	80g	"	"	"
Onion bhajis	2	50g	5 minutes	LOW	Low metal Rack
Onion bhajis	4	110g	7 minutes	LOW	Low metal Rack
Samosas	4	200g	7 minutes	LOW	Low metal Rack
Spring rolls	2	—	See Dual Cook Reheating Chart (Page 26)		
Spring rolls	4	—	"	"	"
Fruit pie Small	2	50g	See Microwave/Dual Cook Reheating Charts (Pages 25, 26)		
	4	100g	"	"	"
Fruit pie Large	1	545g	See Microwave Reheating Chart (Page 25)		

DUAL COOK AND DUAL GRILL
1. For small items it may be necessary to place them on a heatproof dish on the metal rack. This will also help prevent arcing in the oven.
2. Allow to stand for 30 seconds-2 minutes depending on the item of food.

The reheating times are a rough guide only as the initial temperature of the food will affect the required reheating times.

REHEATING CHARTS FOR TINNED FOODS

FOOD	WEIGHT Kg/g	lb. oz	MINUTES ON HIGH
Tinned meats			
Beef and kidney	390	13½ oz	3½ minutes
Stewed steak	410	14½ oz	3½ minutes
Irish stew	390	13½ oz	3½ minutes
Minced beef + onion	390	13½ oz	3½ minutes
Beef casserole	400	14 oz	4 minutes
Meat balls in tomato sauce	415	14½ oz	4 minutes
Chilli con carne	420	14½ oz	4 minutes
Lamb curry	370	13 oz	4 minutes
Scottish mince	430	15½ oz	4 minutes
Lamb hot pot	400	14 oz	4 minutes
Beef madras	230	8 oz	2 minutes
Minced beef + onions	200	7 oz	2 minutes
4 beefburgers + gravy	425	15 oz	4 minutes
10 hot dogs in brine	410	14½ oz	3½ minutes
Tinned meat puddings			
Fray Bentos			
Steak + kidney pudding	210	7½ oz	3 minutes
Steak + kidney pudding	425	15 oz	4 minutes

	WEIGHT kg/g	MICROWAVE POWER	CONVECTION	COOKING TIME
Tinned meat pies				
Plumrose:				
Beef with stout pie	425	MED/LOW	200°C	15 minutes
Tyne:				
Chicken + vegetable pie	430	MED/LOW	200°C	15 minutes

	WEIGHT Kg/g	lb. oz	MINUTES ON HIGH
Tinned vegetables			
Artichoke Hearts	300	10½ oz	3½ minutes
Asparagus spears	340	12 oz	3½ minutes
Beans, Butter	210	7½ oz	2 minutes
Green	410	14½ oz	3½ minutes
Haricot (verts)	400	14 oz	3½ minutes
Re-fried	450	1 lb	5 minutes
Brussels sprouts	400	14 oz	3½ minutes
Cabbage red	400	14 oz	3½ minutes
Carrots, Sliced	425	15 oz	4 minutes
Whole	400	14 oz	4 minutes
Celery, Chopped	410	14½ oz	4 minutes
Whole	400	14 oz	4 minutes

REHEATING CHARTS
FOR TINNED FOODS (CONT.)

FOOD	WEIGHT Kg/g	lb. oz	MINUTE ON HIGH
Corn baby	425	15 oz	4 minutes
Mushrooms, Button	280	10 oz	3 minutes
Creamed	210	7½ oz	3½ minutes
Onions chopped	300	10½ oz	3 minutes
Peas	145	5 oz	1½ minutes
	300	10½ oz	3 minutes
	540	1lb 4 oz	4 minutes
Chick	400	14 oz	4 minutes
Mushy	145	5 oz	2 minutes
	300	10½ oz	3½ minutes
Pudding	440	15½ oz	5 minutes
Potatoes new	400	14 oz	4 minutes
	540	1 lb 4 oz	4½ minutes
Spinach, chopped	400	14 oz	3½ minutes
Sweetcorn	200	7 oz	2 minutes
	300	10½ oz	3 minutes
Tomatoes	210	7½ oz	2½ minutes
	400	14 oz	3½ minutes
Vegetables mixed	300	10½ oz	4 minutes
Pasta			
Ravioli in tomato + meat sauce	200	7 oz	3 minutes
	430	15½ oz	4 minutes
Chicken ravioli	200	7 oz	3 minutes
	430	15½ oz	4 minutes
Spaghetti in tomato sauce	215	7½ oz	3 minutes
	425	15 oz	4 minutes
Spaghetti bolognese	210	7½ oz	3 minutes
	430	15½ oz	4 minutes
Maccaroni cheese	210	7½ oz	3 minutes
	430	15½ oz	4 minutes
Cannelloni in tomato sauce	400	14 oz	4 minutes
Spaghetti hoops	210	7½ oz	3 minutes
	425	15 oz	4 minutes
Beans			
Baked beans	225	8 oz	3 minutes
	450	1 lb	4 minutes
Baked beans + 4 pork sausages	225	8 oz	3 minutes
+ 8 pork sausages	450	1 lb	4 minutes
Baked beans + beefburgers	440	15½ oz	4 minutes
Ghostbusters	210	7½ oz	3 minutes
Postman Pat	425	15 oz	4 minutes

REHEATING CHARTS
FOR TINNED FOODS (CONT.)

| FOOD | WEIGHT | | MINUTE |
	Kg/g	lb. oz	ON HIGH
Soups			
Cream soup (tomato)	290	10½ oz	3 minutes
	425	15 oz	4 minutes
Thick soup (vegetable)	300	10½ oz	3½ minutes
	435	10½ oz	4½ minutes
Thin soup (oxtail)	290	10½ oz	3 minutes
	425	15 oz	4 minutes
Vegetable soup	300	10½ oz	3 minutes
	435	15½ oz	4 minutes
Desserts			
Tinned puddings:			
Creamed rice pudding	170	6 oz	1½ minutes
	425	15 oz	3½ minutes
Maccaroni pudding	425	15 oz	3½ minutes
Semolina pudding	425	15 oz	3½ minutes
Tapioca pudding	425	15 oz	3½ minutes
Custard	425	15 oz	3½ minutes
Dessert custard	425	15 oz	3½ minutes
Chocolate sponge	300	10½ oz	2 minutes
Treacle sponge	300	10½ oz	2 minutes

CONVERSION CHARTS
(Approximate)

OVEN TEMPERATURES			LIQUID EQUIVALENTS		WEIGHT	
°F	°C	Gas Mark			Metric gms	Imperial oz
225	110	¼	1 fl oz	30 millilitres	25g	1oz
250	130	½	¼pt	150 millilitres	50g	2oz
275	140	1	½pt	300 millilitres	100g	4oz
300	150	2	¾pt	445 millilitres	175g	6oz
325	170	3	1pt	600 millilitres	225g	8oz
350	180	4	1¾pt approx.	1 litre	350g	12oz
375	190	5			450g	16oz
400	200	6				
425	220	7				
450	230	8				

SOUPS AND STARTERS

Minestrone Soup

1. Sauté the onion, margarine, leek and bacon together for 5 minutes on HIGH in a large bowl covered.
2. Add all other ingredients with the stock and stir.
3. Cook for 5 minutes on HIGH, then 25-28 minutes on MEDIUM.
4. Cover and allow to stand for 10 minutes.

1 medium onion - peeled and chopped
1 medium leek - chopped
100g (4oz) smoked streaky bacon - chopped
25g (1oz) margarine
1 medium carrot - chopped
100g (4oz) swede - chopped
400g (14oz) tin tomatoes - chopped
50g (2oz) quick cook macaroni
900ml (1 1/2pt) boiling beef stock
1/4 x 5ml (1/4 tsp) ground black pepper
1/2 x 5ml (1/2 tsp) salt
1/2 x 5ml (1/2 tsp) oregano

French Onion Soup

1. Place onions, butter, 600ml (1pt) of stock into a large bowl. Cook for 17-20 minutes on HIGH.
2. Stir in remaining stock and Worcester sauce and season to taste.
3. Cook for 4-5 minutes on HIGH. Stand before serving.

350g (12oz onion - thinly sliced
1200ml (2pt) hot beef stock (using 3 stock cubes)
25g (1oz) butter
1 x 15ml (1 tbsp) Worcester sauce
salt and pepper

Creamy Tomato and Carrot Soup

1. In a large non-metallic casserole dish melt the butter for 1 minute on HIGH.
2. Add onion, and garlic cook for 2 minutes on HIGH.
3. Add the carrots and tomatoes, stir and cook for 5 minutes on HIGH.
4. Mix together the water and cornflour, pour onto the carrots and onion mixture. Stir in the thyme, chicken stock and seasoning mix well and cook for 8-10 minutes on HIGH.
5. Remove from oven, liquidise well, stir in the double cream - reheat if required for 1 minute on HIGH.

1 onion - peeled and chopped
225g (8oz) carrots - peeled and grated
25g (1oz) butter
3 x 15ml (3 tbsp) water
25g (1oz) cornflour
375g (13oz) tomatoes - skinned and roughly chopped
1 clove garlic - peeled and chopped
1 x 5ml (1 tsp) fresh or dried thyme
450ml (3/4pt) chicken stock
4 x 15ml (4 tbsp) double cream
seasoning

Lentil Soup

1. Place lentils, onions, carrot and stock in a large bowl.
2. Cook for 20-25 minutes on HIGH, covered, stir halfway through cooking.
3. Season and liquidise until smooth. Reheat for 2-3 minutes before serving.

225g (8oz) lentils - soaked
2 medium onions - chopped
1 medium carrot - chopped
750ml (1 1/4pt) bacon stock (water and 2 bacon rashers)
seasoning

25g (1oz) butter
1 onion-peeled and finely chopped
2 garlic cloves - roughly chopped
225g (8oz) peeled prawns
100g (4oz) button mushroom - sliced
2 x 15ml (2 tbsp) dry white wine
50g (2oz) cream cheese
100g (4oz) sour cream
1 x 15ml (1 tbsp) cornflour
50g (2oz) cheddar cheese - grated
1 x 5ml (1 tsp) sweet paprika
seasoning

Prawn and Mushroom Ramekins

1. Place butter in a microwaveable dish and heat for 1 minute on HIGH. Add onion and garlic and heat for 2 minutes on HIGH.
2. Add peeled prawns and mushrooms. Mix well and cook for 2 minutes on HIGH.
3. Mix cream cheese, sour cream and salt and pepper together.
4. Mix together white wine and cornflour to make a smooth paste. Add this to cream cheese mixture.
5. Mix together cheese mix and prawns.
6. Divide equally between 4 microwaveable ramekin dishes. Sprinkle paprika and then cheese over prawn mix.
7. Place on high metal rack and cook on DUAL COOK GRILL (microwave MED-LOW/GRILL) for 6-7 minutes.

4 slices bread - lightly toasted
25g (1oz) butter
175g (6oz) cheddar cheese
1/4 x 5ml (1/4 tsp) ground mace
pinch of powdered mustard
2 1/2 x 15ml (2 1/2 tbsp) beer
seasoning

Welsh Rarebit

1. Butter the toast whilst still hot.
2. In a non-metallic bowl place the cheese, ground mace, pinch of powdered mustard and beer.
3. Heat for 1-2 minutes on HIGH until melted.
4. Mix well until thick and creamy. Season to taste.
5. Spread the mixture on the toast.
6. Place the toast on the high metal rack. Place under the grill for 4-6 minutes, until slightly golden.

225g (8oz) broccoli florets
225g (8oz) cauliflower florets
225g (8oz) carrots - peeled and sliced
15ml (1 tbsp) celery tops - finely chopped
3 x size 3 eggs
175g (6oz) cream cheese
salt and pepper

Vegetable Terrine

1. Lightly grease a 2pt microwaveable loaf dish.
2. Place broccoli florets in microwaveable dish with 1 tbsp of water. Cover, vent and cook for 4 1/2-5 minutes on HIGH. Repeat this with cauliflower and carrots.
3. Separate eggs. Beat yolks with cream cheese until smooth. Season. Beat egg whites until they form stiff peaks. Fold whites into cream cheese mixture.
4. Purée each of the vegetables separately.
5. Add one third of egg mixture to broccoli and fold. Repeat this with cauliflower. Add finely chopped celery tops to carrot and then fold in remaining egg.
6. Pour broccoli mixture into loaf dish, smooth surface. Pour over cauliflower purée and smooth. Repeat with carrot mixture. Cover with microwave plastic wrap and vent.
7. Place loaf container into a larger dish containing 1pt of boiling water. Place both dishes on low rack and cook for 12-13 minutes on MED-LOW until set.
8. Allow to cool in dish. Turn out and serve.

Garlic Prawns

225g (8oz) prawns
100g (4oz) butter
1 large clove garlic - crushed
1 x 15ml (1 tbsp) parsley - chopped

1. Melt the butter in a large dish for 1 minute on HIGH.
2. Add the garlic, prawns and parsley. Cook for 1 minute on HIGH.
3. Serve hot in individual dishes.

Coquilles St Jacques

225g (8oz) unshelled scallops
50g (2oz) button mushrooms
3 spring onions - chopped finely
1 stick of celery - chopped finely
3 x 15ml (3 tbsp) plain flour
75g (3oz) butter
150ml (¼pt) white wine
2 x 15ml (2 tbsp) double cream
225g (8oz) mashed potato (mixed with 1 egg yolk)
seasoning

1. Cook scallops for 3-3½ minutes on HIGH.
2. Drain and reserve liquid.
3. Melt butter for 1 minute on HIGH.
4. Add mushrooms, celery and spring onions to butter and cook for 30 seconds on HIGH.
5. Add flour, stir well and cook for 30 seconds on HIGH.
6. Make wine up to 300ml (½pt) with liquid from the scallops. Blend in with the flour.
7. Cook for 3-4 minutes until sauce thickens, stir once during cooking, then stir in the cream. Season to taste. Chop up scallops and add to the sauce.
8. Divide the sauce between four dishes and pipe potato round the edges of each dish.
9. Place on high metal rack. Brown the potato by placing under the grill for 5-7 minutes.

1.5kg (3 lb) mussels
1 onion - chopped
150ml (¹/₄pt) white wine
150ml (¹/₄pt) water
2 x 15ml (2 tbsp) cornflour
2 x 15ml (2 tbsp) double cream
seasoning

Mussels in White Wine

1. Clean mussels removing beards and barnacles.
2. Place wine, water and onion in a large bowl and cook for 2 minutes on HIGH.
3. Add mussels and cook on HIGH in a covered dish for 7-9 minutes until all the shells are open. Discard any shells which do not open. Stir well during cooking.
4. Drain mussels and reserve liquid.
5. Mix a little of the liquid with the cornflour to form a smooth paste. Add to the rest of the liquid.
6. Heat for 5-6 minutes on HIGH, until the sauce thickens, stirring twice during cooking.
7. Stir in cream. Season to taste. Pour over mussels.

1 x 175g (6oz) pkt frozen kipper fillets
25g (1oz) butter
ground black pepper and salt
1 x 15ml (1 tbsp) chopped parsley
200g (7oz) cream cheese
1 x 5ml (1 tsp) lemon juice

Kipper Pâté

1. Pierce the bag of kippers. Heat for 2 minutes on HIGH. Stand for 5 minutes. Heat for further 2-3½ minutes on HIGH.
2. Skin the fillets, remove bones and flake fish. Mash well or place in a liquidiser.
3. Place butter in a small dish, and melt for 40 seconds on HIGH. Blend in cream cheese, lemon juice and chopped parsley. Add kippers to the remaining ingredients and mix well. Season to taste. Spoon into individual ramekins.

12 medium open mushrooms - washed
75g (3oz) butter
50g (2oz) breadcrumbs
1 x 5ml (1 tsp) garlic granules.

Garlic Stuffed Mushrooms

1. Carefully cut the stalks out of the mushrooms and chop the stalks finely.
2. Melt butter for 1½ minutes on HIGH.
3. Stir in breadcrumbs, garlic and chopped mushroom stalks.
4. Divide the mixture between the mushrooms, filling the open centre. Cook for 3-3½ minutes on HIGH or until the mushrooms are soft. Serve hot.

450g (1 lb) spare ribs
5 x 15ml (5 tbsp) Cola
5 x 15ml (5 tbsp) tomato sauce

Quick Barbequed Spare Ribs

1. Cook spare ribs for 8-10 minutes on HIGH. Drain off fat.
2. Mix cola and tomato sauce together and pour over ribs.
3. Cook for 14-19 minutes on DUAL COOK BAKE (on 200°C microwave MED-LOW), placed on low rack, until the fat is crispy, basting with the sauce two or three times.

Devilled Kidneys

450g (1 lb) kidneys, membranes and
cores removed and sliced
25g (1oz) butter
1 small onion - finely chopped
1 x 15ml (1 tbsp) dry sherry
1 x 15ml (1 tbsp) Worcestershire sauce
1 x 15ml (1 tbsp) parsley - if required
½ x 5ml (½ tsp) mustard
½ x 5ml (½ tsp) cornflour

1. Heat the butter in a casserole dish for 30 seconds on HIGH.
2. Add the onions and cook for 3 minutes on HIGH. Stirring half way through the cooking time.
3. Stir in the sliced kidneys. Cover and cook for 2 minutes on HIGH.
4. Stir re-cover then cook for 2 minutes on HIGH.
5. Add the dry sherry, Worcestershire sauce, mustard and parsley - if required. Season to taste. Cover and cook for 1 minute on HIGH.
6. Pour off a little of the juices from the cooked kidneys. Blend with the cornflour to form a smooth paste.
7. Pour back into the kidney mixture. Stir well. Cook for 2-3 minutes on HIGH. Stirring half way through the cooking time.
8. Serve with toast.

Mushroom Soup

175g (6oz) mushrooms
750ml (1¼pt) chicken stock
1 medium onion - chopped
150ml (¼pt) single cream
25g (1oz) margarine
salt and pepper
2 x 15ml (2 tbsp) cornflour
4 x 15ml (4 tbsp) water

1. Place mushrooms, onions, and margarine in a large bowl. Cook for 2 minutes on HIGH.
2. Add stock and cook for 7-8 minutes on HIGH.
3. Thicken with cornflour.
4. Cook for 1 minute on HIGH. Then liquidise.
5. Stir in 150ml (¼pt) single cream.
6. Reheat for 2-3 minutes on HIGH.

FISH

Scampi Provençal

225g (8oz) scampi
400g (14oz) tinned tomatoes - drained
1 onion chopped
2 cloves garlic - crushed
25g (1oz) butter
seasoning

1. In a casserole dish place the butter, onions and garlic together. Cook for 3 minutes on HIGH.
2. Chop the drained tomatoes. Add to the cooked onion, also add the scampi. Cook for 6-8 minutes on HIGH, until the scampi is tender. Season to taste. Serve with rice.

Sole Bonne Femme

450g (1 lb) lemon sole
37g (1½oz) plain flour
150ml (¼pt) milk
25g (1oz) butter
juice of 1 lemon
small bunch of green grapes - stoned
seasoning

1. Roll up each piece of sole, skin side inwards. Place in a dish.
2. Cover and cook for 6-7 minutes on HIGH.
3. Place the butter in a bowl. Melt for 30 seconds on HIGH. Stir in the flour.
4. Gradually add the milk. Cook for 3-4 minutes on HIGH. Whisk half way through the cooking time.
5. Add the lemon juice, grapes and juice from the fish.
6. Pour the sauce over the fish. Serve.

Sussex Skate Wings

1 leek - cut into thin strips
50g (2oz) butter
4 x 15ml (4 tbsp) dry white wine
2 x 15ml (2 tbsp) capers
450g (1 lb) skate wings
salt and pepper

1. Place 25g (1oz) of the butter in a bowl. Melt for 30 seconds on HIGH.
2. Add the white wine, seasoning and leeks. Cook for 2½-3 minutes on HIGH. Add the capers. Set aside.
3. Melt the remaining butter, in a dish for 1 minute on HIGH.
4. Brush the melted butter over the skate.
5. Place the skate on a dish, with the thinner part to the centre of the dish.
6. Cover and cook for 5-6 minutes on HIGH.
7. Leave to stand for 4 minutes.
8. Re-heat the sauce for 1 minute on HIGH. Pour the juices from the fish into the sauce. Season with salt and pepper.
9. Arrange the skate on a serving dish.
10. Pour the sauce over the skate and serve.

700g (1½ lb) potatoes - peeled and
chopped
37g (1½oz) margarine
37g (1½oz) flour
300ml (½pt) milk
2 fish fillets e.g. cod
25g (1oz) cheese - grated
For the potatoes
50g (2oz) butter
4 x 15ml (4 tbsp) milk

Fish Pie

1. Melt the margarine in a bowl for 1 minute on HIGH.
2. Add the flour. Gradually add the milk.
3. Cook for 3 minutes on HIGH. Stirring half way through the cooking time. Whisk until smooth. Season to taste.
4. Cover and cook the fish for 3-3½ minutes on HIGH. Flake the fish and mix with the sauce. Pour into a dish.
5. Place the potatoes in a dish, add 5 x 15ml (5 tbsp) of water. Cover and cook for 8-10 minutes on HIGH until soft enough to mash.
6. Mash the potatoes with the butter and milk. Place on top of the fish sauce.
7. Sprinkle the cheese on top of the potatoes.
8. Place on high metal rack and cook for 6-7 minutes DUAL COOK GRILL (microwave MED-HIGH/GRILL).

2 medium trout (225g (8oz) each)
25g (1oz) flaked almonds
juice of 1 orange
thin slices of orange for garnish
seasoning

Trout with Almonds and Orange

1. Wash trout, place in a dish and season.
2. Pour over the orange juice and sprinkle with flaked almonds.
3. Cook for 4-5 minutes on HIGH, covered.
4. Garnish with orange slices and parsley.

2 x 15ml (2 tbsp) vegetable oil
1 onion - roughly chopped
1 carrot - cut into sticks
1 x 15ml (1 tbsp) curry powder
25g (1oz) mushrooms - quartered
½ green pepper - cut into strips
100g (4oz) pineapple - chopped
150ml (¼pt) chicken stock
2 x 15ml (2 tbsp) cornflour (mixed
with 2 x 15ml (2 tbsp) stock)
100g (4oz) peeled prawns
seasoning

Prawn Curry

1. In a casserole dish, heat the veg oil, 1 minute on MED-HIGH.
2. Add onion and curry powder and cook 2 minutes on HIGH.
3. Add carrot, pepper, mushrooms, pineapple and stock and cook 5-6 minutes on HIGH.
4. Stir in prawns and cornflour paste. Return to oven for 2-3 minutes on HIGH.
5. Serve with rice and lemon wedges.

225g (8oz) button mushrooms -
chopped
100g (4oz) tomatoes - peeled and
chopped
100g (4oz) onion - chopped
2 x 15ml (2 tbsp) chopped parsley
mixed herbs to taste
8 plaice fillets (approx. 450g (1 lb) -
skinned)
seasoning

Stuffed Plaice Fillets

1. Mix together the mushrooms, tomatoes, onion, parsley and mixed herbs, salt and pepper in a bowl. Cook for 5 minutes on HIGH. Place equal amounts of the mixture on each fillet and roll up.
2. Arrange fillets in a dish and remaining mixture around them.
3. Cover and cook for 7-9 minutes on HIGH.

Fish Timbale

1. In a non-metallic dish heat butter for 1 minute on HIGH.
2. Add the onion and cook for 1 minute on HIGH.
3. Stir in curry powder, flaked almonds and add rice. Mix well then pour over ³/₄pt hot water. Season to taste.
4. Cook for 12-15 minutes on HIGH - stirring half way through cooking. Stir and allow to stand for 1-2 minutes.
5. For the fish mixture, melt the butter for 30 seconds on HIGH. Add the onion, chopped mushrooms, tinned salmon/tuna, celery and sweetcorn. Mix well.
6. Cook for 5-6 minutes on HIGH.
7. Mix the rice mixture and fish mixture together. Season to taste. Allow mixture to cool slightly.
8. Lightly grease a 2pt pudding basin. Roll out three quarters of the puff pastry and line the pudding basin (allow enough to fold back over the top of the filling).
9. Pour in the filling, fold back the remaining pastry and brush with melted butter.
10. Roll out remaining one quarter of pastry to fit over the top of the pastry. Trim edges and brush with melted butter.
11. Cook for 20 minutes on DUAL COOK (on 200°C microwave LOW).

225g (8oz) puff pastry
15g (¹/₂oz) melted butter

For the rice:
200g (7oz) long grain rice
50g (2oz) butter
1 onion - peeled and chopped
2 x 5ml (2 tsp) curry powder seasoning
50g (2oz) almonds - flaked
450ml (³/₄pt) hot water

Fish Mixture
25g (1oz) butter
1 onion - peeled and chopped
175g (6oz) mushrooms - chopped
225g (8oz) tinned salmon/tuna (liquid drained)
1 stick of celery - sliced
50g (2oz) sweetcorn

Halibut Steaks with Tomatoes and Cream

1. Place fish steaks in a casserole dish and cook for 10-12 minutes on HIGH.
2. In a medium sized bowl melt the butter for 1 minute on HIGH. Add onions and cook for 2-3 minutes on HIGH. Add the cornflour mix well.
3. Add remaining ingredients. Cook for 5 minutes on HIGH. Stir halfway through. Add cream, cook for 1 minute on HIGH. Stir well.
4. Pour over the halibut steaks. Reheat for 1-2 minutes on HIGH if required.

25g (1oz) butter
1 large onion - thinly sliced and separated into rings
1 x 400g (14oz) can tomatoes - chopped
1 x 5ml (1 tsp) dried marjoram
¹/₂ x 5ml (¹/₂ tsp) salt
¹/₄ x 5ml (¹/₄ tsp) black pepper
4 halibut steaks (225g (8oz) each)
225g (8oz) button mushrooms halved
150ml (¹/₄pt) double cream
1 x 15ml (1 tbsp) cornflour

Cod with Parsley Sauce

1. Place fish into a serving dish, cover and cook for 4-5 minutes on HIGH. Allow to stand.
2. Put the margarine in a 1 litre (2pt) bowl or jug and heat for 1 minute on HIGH or until melted. Stir in flour and milk. Heat for 3¹/₂-4 minutes on HIGH until creamy. Whisk until smooth.
3. Stir in chopped parsley.
4. Pour over cooked fish, garnish, and serve.

450g (1 lb) cod steaks
300ml (¹/₂pt) milk
25g (1oz) flour
25g (1oz) margarine
15g (¹/₂oz) chopped parsley

FISH

450g (1 lb) smoked haddock
25g (1oz) butter
25g (1oz) flour
300ml (½pt) milk
2 x 15ml (2 tbsp) orange juice and rind
25g (1oz) capers - chopped
1 x 15ml (1 tbsp) double cream
salt and pepper

Smoked Haddock in Caper and Orange Sauce

1. Place the fish in a dish and cover. Cook for 5-6 minutes on HIGH.
2. Melt the butter in a bowl for 30 seconds on HIGH. Stir in the flour.
3. Gradually add the milk.
4. Cook for 3 minutes on HIGH. Stir half way through the cooking time. Season to taste.
5. Pour the juices from the fish into the sauce. Add the capers, orange rind, cream and orange juice. Season to taste.
6. Pour the sauce over the fish.

2 x 15ml (2 tbsp) olive oil
1 garlic clove - peeled and crushed
1 onion - peeled and chopped
200g (7oz) long grain rice
600ml (1pt) chicken stock
½ x 5ml (½ tsp) turmeric
1 red pepper - seeded and sliced
100g (4oz) prawns
100g (4oz) mange tout
100g (4oz) cockles - cooked
100g (4oz) baby corn
100g (4oz) mussels - cooked
225g (8oz) chicken - cooked and sliced
seasoning

Paella

1. In a non-metallic bowl place garlic, oil and onion and cook on HIGH for 2 minutes.
2. Add the stock, rice, turmeric and seasoning to taste. Stir well then cook uncovered for 9-11 minutes on HIGH until the rice is tender stirring two or three times throughout cooking. Let the rice stand for 2-3 minutes.
3. Place mange tout, corn and peppers in a non-metallic dish. Add 2 x 15ml (2 tbsp) water. Cover and cook on HIGH for 2-3 minutes.
4. Add remaining ingredients and vegetables, toss and reheat for 4-5 minutes on HIGH. Stir half way through the cooking time.

4 herrings

Sauce:
225g (8oz) gooseberries
90ml (6 tbsp) water
1-2 x 5ml (1-2 tsp) sugar (to taste)
1 x 15ml spoon (1 tbsp) chopped dill

Herrings in Gooseberry Sauce

1. Place herrings in a dish and cover, cook for 6-7 minutes on HIGH per 450g (1 lb).
2. Make the sauce by placing all of the ingredients together, cover and cook for 4-5 minutes on HIGH, stirring half way through the cooking time.
3. Purée the gooseberries.
4. Serve with the herrings.

450g (1 lb) filleted fish
25g (1oz) butter
3 x 15ml (3 tbsp) milk or white wine
black pepper

Poached Fish

1. Arrange fish in a large shallow dish. Dot the surface with butter, pour over wine and sprinkle with pepper.
2. Cover dish and cook for 4-5 minutes on HIGH. Leave to stand.

Beef en Croûte

1kg (2 lb) fillet beef
450g (1 lb) puff pastry
50g (2oz) smooth pâté
1 x size 3 egg - beaten
100g (4oz) mushrooms - chopped

1. Place the beef on the low metal rack and cook for 8-11 minutes on MEDIUM. The meat will be very rare, but during standing it will continue to cook so beware of over cooking.
2. Cut the pastry in half and roll out 2.5cm (1″) larger than the beef, all the way round. Place pastry on a baking sheet and brush edges with beaten egg.
3. Place meat on top of pastry and spread pâté and chopped mushrooms over the meat.
4. Roll out remaining half of the pastry, large enough to completely cover top and sides of beef. Cut to fit.
5. Seal down edges of top and bottom layers of pastry. Coat all over with beaten egg.
6. Pastry decorations can be made with any remaining pastry. Place on top of pastry cover and brush with egg. Place on low rack.
7. Cook for 17-20 minutes on DUAL COOK (on 200°C microwave MED-LOW) or until the pastry is golden brown and crispy.
   Madeira sauce would be a suitable accompaniment to this dish.

Beef with Broccoli and Oyster Sauce

450g (1 lb) fillet steak - sliced
225g (8oz) fresh broccoli - chopped
1 red pepper - seeded and sliced
1 yellow pepper - seeded and sliced
2 x 15ml (2 tbsp) vegetable oil
1 x bottle oyster sauce
2 x 5ml (2 tsp) cornflour
seasoning

1. In a casserole dish heat the oil for 30 seconds on HIGH.
2. Add the sliced steak, cook for 2½ minutes on HIGH.
3. In a bowl place the peppers, broccoli and water. Cover and cook for 2 minutes on HIGH.
4. Reserve water from the cooked vegetables. Add vegetables to sliced steak. Cook for 2½ minutes on HIGH. Blend the cornflour with the reserved water.
5. Stir oyster sauce and cornflour mixture into beef and vegetables. Cook for a further 2½ minutes on HIGH. Stirring halfway through. Season to taste.

Lamb Curry

175g (6oz) onions - peeled and chopped
25g (1oz) margarine or butter
350g (12oz) lamb - cubed
25g (1oz) flour - seasoned
1 cooking apple - peeled, cored and chopped
450ml (¾pt) hot water
1 stock cube
50g (2oz) sultanas
2 x 15ml (2 tbsp) curry powder
50g (2oz) creamed coconut

1. Place chopped onions and margarine or butter and cook for 2 minutes on HIGH.
2. Place the diced lamb in the bowl, add the seasoned flour, toss. Cook for 4-5 minutes on HIGH, stirring half way through.
3. Add the curry powder. Cook for 1 minute on HIGH.
4. Add the apple, sultanas and creamed coconut. Dissolve the stock cube in the hot water. Add to other ingredients.
5. Cover and cook for 10 minutes on HIGH and for 35 minutes on MED-LOW.

450g (1 lb) best quality steak - cubed
25g (1oz) seasoned flour
225g (8oz) onions - chopped
2 peppers - seeded and sliced
25g (1oz) oil
2 x 5ml (2 tsp) paprika
3 x 15ml (3 tbsp) tomato paste
seasoning
25g (1oz) plainflour
2 tomatoes - skinned and quartered
1 bouquet garni
450ml (¾pt) red wine and water

For the dumplings
100g (4oz) self raising flour
50 g (2oz) suet
water to mix
1-2 x 15ml (1-2 tbsp) caraway seeds

Goulash with Dumplings

1. Coat the meat with seasoned flour.
2. Place onions and pepper with oil and paprika in a casserole dish. Cover and cook for 2 minutes on HIGH.
3. Add the meat and cook for 6-7 minutes on HIGH until brown.
4. Add the remaining ingredients. (Except the 25g (1oz) flour) to the casserole.
5. Cover and cook for 30 minutes on DUAL COOK (on 180°C microwave MEDIUM). Stirring twice during cooking.
6. Mix in the remaining 25g (1oz) flour. Cook for 5 minutes on HIGH, Stir well.
7. Mix flour, suet and caraway seeds for the dumplings. Add water to mix. Form into 4 dumplings
8. Place dumplings on top of goulash. Place on the high metal rack. Cook for 6 minutes DUAL COOK GRILL (microwave MEDIUM/GRILL)

450g (1 lb) best quality steak - cubed
100g (4oz) ox kidney - cubed
1 onion - chopped
½ x 5ml (½ tsp) mixed herbs
2 x 15ml (2 tbsp) cornflour
400ml (¾pt) water
Pastry:
225g (8oz) self raising flour
½ x 5ml (½ tsp) salt
1 x 5ml (1 tsp) baking powder
100g (4oz) shredded suet
approx 125-150ml (¼pt) cold
water

Steak and Kidney Pudding

1. Place steak, kidney, chopped onion, herbs and water in a casserole dish.
2. Cover and cook for 40-45 minutes on MEDIUM LOW, stirring half way through cooking. Add cornflour to thicken the juices 2 minutes before the end of cooking.
3. Meanwhile, make the pastry by sieving flour, salt and baking powder together in a bowl.
4. Stir in suet and mix to a soft dough with cold water. Knead lightly.
5. Roll out ⅔ rds of the pastry and line a 1 litre (1¾pt) well greased pudding basin. Roll out remaining pastry into a circle.
6. Allow meat to stand for 10 minutes before filling pudding basin, cover with a circle of pastry. Moisten top of pastry. Make slit in the top to allow steam to escape. Cover with kitchen paper and cook for 10-12 minutes on MEDIUM.
7. Stand for 6 minutes.

450g (1 lb) minced beef
1 x size 3 egg - beaten
1½ x 5ml (1½ tsp) chilli powder
seasoning

Tomato sauce:
1 onion - chopped
1 clove garlic - chopped
1 x 15ml (1 tbsp) oil
400g (14oz) tin tomatoes
1 x 15ml (1 tbsp) basil, chopped

Meatballs in Tomato Sauce

1. Mix together minced beef, egg, chilli powder and seasoning. Form into 14 small balls.
2. Place on a plate and cook for 8-9 minutes on HIGH. The meat balls will need re-arranging during the cooking time.
3. Heat the oil for 1 minute on HIGH.
4. Add onion and garlic. Cook for 3 minutes on HIGH. Then add tomatoes, basil and seasoning, cook for 6 minutes on HIGH. Then purée.
5. Transfer cooked meatballs onto a serving dish and pour over the tomato sauce.

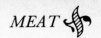

Leg of Lamb in Redcurrant Sauce

220g (1 jar) redcurrant jelly
300ml (½pt) red wine
1 x 5ml (1 tsp) dijon mustard
4 cloves garlic - sliced into chunks
seasoning
1 joint of lamb

1. Mix the redcurrant jelly, red wine, dijon mustard and seasoning together in a large heatproof non-metallic dish.
2. Heat the redcurrant jelly, red wine and dijon mustard for 2 minutes on HIGH. Mix well to dissolve the redcurrant jelly.
3. Place the leg of lamb in the liquid and marinade for 1 hour (turn over half way through).
4. Make a few small slices into the skin of the lamb. Insert the garlic cloves into the skin.
5. Place the non-metallic dish on the low metal rack. Cook for 14-15 minutes per 450g/ 1 lb, DUAL COOK (on 160°C microwave MEDIUM) basting and turning over throughout cooking.

Beef Carbonade

1 medium onion - peeled and sliced
2 x 15ml (2 tbsp) oil
25g (1oz) plainflour
700g (1½ lb) stewing steak - cubed
1 beef stock cube
300ml (½pt) boiling water
300ml (½pt) beer or stout
1 bouquet garni
seasoning
6 x 2½ (1") slices French bread
1 x 15ml (1 tbsp) English mustard

1. Place onion and oil into a large microwaveable casserole dish and heat on HIGH for 2 minutes.
2. Add steak and brown on HIGH for 5-6 minutes stirring half-way through cooking time. Stir in flour and mix well.
3. Add boiling water to stock cube. Pour over steak with beer, add bouquet garni and seasoning.
4. Cover with microwaveable lid. Place on low rack and cook on DUAL COOK (on 180°C microwave LOW) stirring once during cooking.
5. Spread one side of each slice of French bread with mustard.
6. Remove casserole lid and place bread slices on top with mustard side upwards.
7. Cook for 3-4 minutes on DUAL COOK GRILL (microwave LOW/GRILL) until bread is golden.

1.3kg (3 lb) oxtail pieces
100g (4oz) swede - diced
1 medium onion - chopped
100g (4oz) celery - chopped
225g (8oz) carrots - sliced
100g (4oz) leeks - sliced
900ml (1½pt) beef stock
salt and pepper to taste

Oxtail Stew

1. Place all the cut vegetables and oxtail in a large 3 litre (6pt) casserole.
2. Add the seasoning to the stock and pour over the vegetables and oxtail. Cover the dish with a lid. Place on low rack.
3. Cook for 1 hr 50 minutes on DUAL COOK (on 160°C microwave MED-LOW). Stir twice during cooking.

1 kg (2 lb 3oz) piece of rolled brisket - tied firmly
6-8 shallot onions - peeled
450g (1 lb) carrots - peeled
400ml (¾pt) of beef stock
salt and pepper to taste
1 bouquet garni

Boiled Beef and Carrots

1. Cut the carrots into even size pieces.
2. Place the meat into a large round 3 litre (6pt) casserole. Arrange the shallot onions and carrot pieces evenly around the meat.
3. Season the beef stock with salt and pepper, and pour over the beef, carrots and onion. Add the bouquet garni to the stock and cover the dish. Place on low rack.
4. Cook for 80 minutes on DUAL COOK (on 160°C microwave MED-LOW). Turn over the meat half way through cooking.
5. If required the juices can be thickened to make a gravy.

8 large cabbage leaves
3 x 15ml (3 tbsp) water
12g (½oz) butter
1 onion - peeled
350g (12oz) minced pork or lamb
1 x 15ml (1 tbsp) parsley
1 x 15ml (1 tbsp) mixed herbs
50g (2oz) breadcrumbs
2½ x 15 ml (2½ tbsp) tomato purée
salt and pepper

Sauce:

1 onion - chopped
1 clove garlic - chopped
1 x 15ml (1 tbsp) oil
400g (14oz) tin of tomatoes - crushed
1 x 15ml (1 tbsp) - basil chopped
seasoning

Stuffed Cabbage Leaves

1. Wash and clean the cabbage leaves.
2. In a bowl add the water and cabbage leaves. Cook for 3-4 minutes on HIGH. Drain.
3. In a dish heat the butter for 30 seconds on HIGH. Add the onions and fry for 4 minutes on HIGH.
4. Mix the minced pork or lamb, parsley, mixed herbs, tomato purée and breadcrumbs. Add the cooked onions. Mix thoroughly.
5. Divide the mixture between the cabbage leaves, place in the centre of each leaf. Roll up each cabbage leaf, by folding both sides, and then roll up from the bottom, to form a parcel. Secure with a cocktail stick.
6. Place the stuffed cabbage leaves in a dish cover and cook for 9-10 minutes on MEDIUM.
7. For the tomato sauce heat the oil for 1 minute on HIGH.
8. Add the onion and garlic. Cook for 3 minutes on HIGH. Stir in the tomatoes, basil and seasoning. Cook for 6 minutes on HIGH.
9. Serve with the stuffed cabbage.

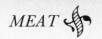

Italian Beef Olives

1. Flatten olives with a rolling pin.
2. Mix together tomatoes, mushrooms, breadcrumbs, tomato purée, shallots, mixed herbs, 45ml (3 tbsp) wine and seasoning. Place equal amounts into the end of each beef olive and roll securely.
3. Place the olives into a dish with edge underneath. Pour over remaining wine. Cook for 18-22 minutes on DUAL COOK (on 200°C microwave MEDIUM) basting 2-3 times during cooking.
4. Remove olives from serving dish. Mix cornflour with 30ml (2 tbsp) of cold water. Stir into beef juices with Madeira. Season. Heat for 1-1½ minutes on microwave HIGH until thickened.
5. Place olives into a serving dish and pour over sauce.

8 beef olives
2 medium tomatoes - cut into small cubes
100g (4oz) mushrooms - sliced
50g (2oz) fresh breadcrumbs
15ml (1 tbsp) tomato purée
2 shallots - finely chopped
1 x 5ml (1 tsp) Italian mixed herbs
6 x 15ml (6 tbsp) red wine
1 x 15ml (1 tbsp) cornflour
1 x 15ml (1 tbsp) Madeira or port (optional)
seasoning

Steak and Kidney Pie

1. Cut up the steak and kidney into a casserole dish. Add the onion and stock. Season and place on low rack. Cover and cook for 25-30 minutes on DUAL COOK (on 180°C microwave MEDIUM).
2. Blend in the cornflour to the stock and meat. Place in a pie dish.
3. Roll out the puff pastry to make the pie lid. Place over filling, damp the edges and trim. Use the trimmings to make pie decorations. Glaze with the egg. Place on low rack.
4. Cook for 10-12 minutes on DUAL COOK (on 200°C microwave MEDIUM).

450g (1 lb) stewing steak and kidney
1 large onion - chopped
450ml (¾pt) beef stock
2 x 15ml (2 tbsp) cornflour
salt and pepper
225g (8oz) puff pastry
1 egg to glaze

1 clove of garlic - chopped
1 onion - chopped
450g (1 lb) minced beef
25g (1oz) butter or margarine
100g (4oz) mushrooms - chopped
1 x 15ml (1 tbsp) tomato purée
1 x 400g (14oz) tin of tomatoes
150ml (¼pt) beef stock
seasoning

Basic Meat Sauce

1. Place the onion, garlic and butter or margarine into a dish. Cook for 2 minutes on HIGH.
2. Add the minced beef and cook for 7 minutes on HIGH - stirring half way through the cooking time.
3. Add the mushrooms, tomato purée tin of tomatoes, beef stock and seasoning.
4. Cook for 20-30 minutes on HIGH, or until the meat sauce has reached a thick consistency.

15g (½oz) margarine
1 large onion
350g (12oz) can corned beef
400g (14oz) can of tomatoes - chopped
½ x 5ml (½ tsp) mixed herbs
2 x 5ml (2 tsp) Worcester sauce
salt and pepper
50g (2oz) bag plain crisps - crushed
25g (1oz) cheese - grated
1 x 397g (14oz) tinned spaghetti

Corned Beef Crisp

1. Melt the margarine in a casserole dish for 1 minute on HIGH.
2. Add the onions and cook for a further 3 minutes on HIGH.
3. Place the cubed corned beef in a casserole dish. Cover with the fried onions, spaghetti, tomatoes, Worcester sauce, mixed herbs, salt and pepper (to taste). Mix lightly.
4. Top with the crushed crisps and grated cheese.
5. Cook for 7-9 minutes on DUAL COOK GRILL (microwave MED-HIGH/GRILL).

5 lamb chops
25g (1oz) stilton - grated
2 spring onions - chopped
1 x 15ml (1 tbsp) red wine
25g (1oz) breadcrumbs
25g (1oz) mushrooms - peeled and chopped
seasoning
5 large sheets of puff pastry
1 x size 3 egg - beaten

Lamb Chops En Croûte

1. Mix all the ingredients together (excluding lamb chops and pastry). Season to taste.
2. Place the lamb chops individually on each pastry sheet placing to one edge so that the pastry can encase the lamb chops.
3. Equally divide the filling mixture and place on top of each lamb chop, spread evenly.
4. Brush the edges of the pastry with the beaten egg and fold the pastry over the chop. Cut around the shape of the lamb chop leaving a 2cm border. Seal edges well. Brush pastry with beaten egg.
5. Place the pastry cutlets onto a lightly greased metal tray.
6. Place onto the low metal rack on turntable.
7. Cook for 18-20 minutes on DUAL COOK (on 200°C microwave MED-LOW).

1 pork loin - boned

Stuffing
2 x 15ml (2 tbsp) English mustard
2 x 15ml (2 tbsp) dijon mustard
3 x 15ml (3 tbsp) parsley (fresh) - chopped
2 x 15ml (2 tbsp) thyme (fresh) - chooped
1 leek - chopped
50g (2oz) breadcrumbs
75g (3oz) pecan nuts - chopped
2 cloves garlic - peeled and chopped

Rolled Mustard Pork

1. Mix all stuffing ingredients together.
2. Spread evenly over the pork.
3. Roll up and tie securely with string.
4. Place on metal baking tray on low metal rack. Cook for 11-13 minutes per 450g/1 lb at DUAL COOK (on 160°C microwave MED) turning over half way through cooking.

Shepherds Pie

1. Place lamb and onion in a large casserole dish and cook, uncovered, on MED-HIGH for 6-7 minutes. Stir in flour and add stock and tomatoes, mix well and season. Add Worcester sauce if required.
2. Cover and cook for 9-11 minutes on MED-HIGH until meat is tender. Allow to stand.
3. Peel and cut potatoes in small pieces. Place in dish with 2 x 15ml (2 tbsp) water. Cover and cook for 6-7 minutes on HIGH, until soft.
4. Cream potatoes with milk and butter, season to taste.
5. Spread over top of meat.
6. Place on high rack and grill for 7-9 minutes until golden brown.
7. Garnish with paprika or chopped parsley.

450g (1 lb) minced lamb
1 small onion - sliced
2 x 15ml (2 tbsp) plain flour
300ml (½pt) stock
2 medium tomatoes - skinned and chopped
salt and pepper
Worcestershire sauce to taste (optional)
Potato topping:
225g (8oz) potatoes
2 x 15ml (2 tbsp) milk
1 x 5ml (1 tsp) butter
seasoning
Garnish:
paprika or chopped parsley

Lancashire Hot Pot

1. Coat the lamb chops with the seasoned flour.
2. Mix together the carrots, onions, celery, leek and mixed herbs, sprinkle with salt and pepper.
3. In a lightly buttered 2.5 litre heat proof casserole dish, place in an even layer half of the sliced potatoes.
4. On top, layer half of the vegetables then place in an even layer the coated lamb chops.
   Place the remaining vegetables on top of the lamb chops.
5. Top with the remaining potato slices, arranging them neatly in overlapping circles.
6. Pour over the beef stock, until the stock reaches the upper potato layer. Brush top of potatoes with oil.
7. Place in the oven and cook for 40-45 minutes on DUAL COOK (on 200°C microwave MED-LOW).

4 lamb chops - fat removed
40g (1½oz) seasoned flour
5 carrots - peeled and sliced
2 medium onions - peeled and chopped
2 sticks celery - chopped
1 leek - peeled and sliced
½ x 5ml (½ tsp) mixed herbs
salt and pepper
4 medium potatoes - peeled and cut into 2cm (¾") thick slices
450ml (¾pt) beef stock

1 lamb shoulder - boned

Marinade

150g (5oz) natural set yoghurt
1 lemon - juice and grated rind
1 x 15ml (1 tbsp) garam masala
2 x 15ml (2 tbsp) fresh chopped mint
3 cloves garlic - crushed
seasoning

Stuffing

100g (4oz) fresh white breadcrumbs
1 x 15ml (1 tbsp) mint (fresh -
chopped)
1 x 5ml (1 tsp) garam masala
1 large onion - peeled and chopped
2 garlic cloves - peeled and chopped

Minted Stuffed Lamb

1. Mix all ingredients together for the marinade. Coat the lamb in marinade. Cover and leave for 1-2 hours (turning over and basting 1-2 times).
2. Remove lamb and spread out flat.
3. To the remaining marinade add the stuffing ingredients. Spread evenly onto the surface of the lamb.
4. Roll lamb up and serve by tying string around the rolled lamb.
5. Place onto a metal baking sheet on the low metal rack.
6. Turn over 1-2 times during cooking (shield if required).

450g (1 lb) pork steak - cubed
1 onion - chopped
25g (1oz) plain flour
25g (1oz) margarine or butter
295g (10.4oz) tin condensed mushroom soup
150ml (¼pt) beef stock
100g (4oz) mushrooms - sliced
seasoning
2 x 15ml (2 tbsp) double cream
1 x 15ml (1 tbsp) brandy

Pork in Brandy and Cream

1. Put pork, onion, flour and margarine or butter in a large casserole dish. Cover and cook for 5 minutes on HIGH, stirring twice during cooking.
2. Add soup, stock, mushrooms and seasoning. Cover and cook for 25-30 minutes on MEDIUM. Stir twice during cooking.
3. Stir in brandy and cream. Adjust seasoning if necessary.

1 onion - chopped
50g (2oz) mushrooms - sliced
1 x 5ml (1 tsp) mixed herbs
225g (8oz) puff pastry
225g (8oz) sausage meat
2 x 15ml (2 tbsp) tomato purée
salt and pepper
egg for glazing

Sausage Plait

1. Place the chopped onion and sliced mushrooms into a heatproof dish and cook for 2 minutes on HIGH.
2. Add the sausage meat and cook for a further 6 minutes on HIGH, add tomato purée, mixed herbs an seasoning to taste and allow to cool.
3. Roll out the pastry to a rectangle 30cm x 15cm (12'' x 6'') trim off the edges make cuts at an angle approximately 5cm (2'') apart.
4. Place the cool filling down the centre of the pastry; taking a strip of pastry from each alternate side. Plait across the filling. Place on a baking sheet and brush with beaten egg. Place on low rack.
5. Cook for 10-13 minutes on DUAL COOK (on 200°C microwave MEDIUM).

450g (1 lb) minced beef
1 large onion - chopped
1 x 400g (14oz) tin tomatoes
1 x 400g (14oz) tin of kidney beans
2 x 15ml (2 tbsp) tomato purée
2-3 x 5ml (2-3 tsp) chilli powder
1 x 15ml (1 tbsp) Worcestershire sauce
1 x beef stock cube
2 fl oz hot water
seasoning

Chilli Con Carne

1. Place minced beef and onion in a casserole dish and cook together for 5 minutes on HIGH.
2. Dissolve beef stock cube in the hot water, and add to mince mixture.
3. Add all remaining ingredients, blend well, cover and cook for 20-25 minutes on MEDIUM.
4. Stand covered for 5-7 minutes.

Honey Glazed Gammon

1.5kg (3 lb) gammon
1 x 15ml (1 tbsp) honey
1 x 15ml (1 tbsp) orange juice
whole cloves

1. Soak gammon overnight in cold water to remove salt.
2. Place the gammon on the low metal rack rind side downwards. Cook for 14-16 minutes per 450g (1 lb) on DUAL COOK (on 160°C microwave MED-HIGH).
3. Halfway through the cooking time turn the joint over. Remove the rind.
4. 10 minutes before the end of cooking score the surface with a sharp knife by taking lines one way and then the other, diagonally to form a diamond shape.
5. Mix honey and orange juice together, stick cloves into each square and brush the honey and orange glaze over the surface.
6. Place back into the oven for the remaining cooking time. Serve hot or cold.

Escalopes of Pork with Sweetcorn Sauce

4 escalopes of pork approx 150g (6oz) each
1 small onion - finely chopped
1 small tin of creamed corn
100g (4oz) sweetcorn kernels
3 x 15ml (3 tbsp) of double cream
salt and pepper to taste
12g (½oz) butter

1. Place the chopped onion and butter in a large casserole dish and cook for 3-4 minutes on HIGH.
2. Place the escalopes of pork in the dish with the onions. Cover and cook for 15-18 minutes on MED-HIGH.
3. Blend the creamed sweetcorn with the double cream. Add the sweetcorn kernels. Season with salt and pepper to taste.
4. Stir the cream mixture into the onions and pork.
5. Cover and cook for 2½-4 minutes on MED-HIGH. Do not allow to boil. Serve.

4 rashers of bacon - streaky
450g (1 lb) lambs liver - thinly sliced
25g (1oz) margarine
25g (1oz) seasoned plain flour
2 tomatoes - skinned and chopped
250ml (½pt) beef stock
parsley
seasoning

Liver and Bacon

1. Cook the bacon for 3 minutes on HIGH.
2. Chop the bacon.
3. Roll the liver in seasoned plain flour.
4. Melt the margarine in a casserole dish on HIGH for 30 seconds.
5. Add the liver, thicken with 1 tbsp cornflour. Cook for a further 2½-3 minutes on HIGH. Stir halfway through.
6. Add bacon, tomatoes and stock. Cook for 4-6 minutes on HIGH. Season to taste. Garnish with chopped parsley.

450g (1 lb) sausages
100g (4oz) plain flour
salt
2 x size 3 eggs - beaten
300ml (½pt) milk

Toad in the Hole

1. Arrange sausages in dish. Place on low metal rack and preheat for 10 minutes on CONVECTION 200°C.
2. Sift salt and flour into a basin. Beat in eggs and milk.
3. Pour the batter over the sausages. Cook for 18-22 minutes on CONVECTION 200°C.

1 carrot - chopped
750g (1½ lb) onions - sliced
2 stalks of celery - chopped
1.15 litre (2pt) hot water
1 bay leaf
6 peppercorns
1 x 15ml (1 tbsp) lemon juice
750g (1½ lb) dressed tripe
75g (3oz) butter or margarine
seasoning
2 x 15ml (2 tbsp) chopped parsley
1-2 x 15ml (1-2 tbsp) cornflour

Tripe and Onions

1. Place the carrot, onions, (225g (½ lb)) celery, bay leaf, peppercorns, lemon juice and water in a bowl.
2. Cover and cook for 10-12 minutes on HIGH. Leave to infuse for 5 minutes.
3. Strain and reserve the liquid.
4. Cut the tripe into thin strips. Place in the bowl with the liquid. Cover and cook for 15-17 minutes on HIGH or until the liquid is boiling.
5. Strain and reserve the tripe - and 600ml (1pt) of stock.
6. In a dish, melt the butter for 1½ minutes on HIGH.
7. Add the remaining sliced onions, cook for 7-9 minutes on HIGH.
8. Add the tripe and parsley. Season to taste. Cook for 3-4 minutes on HIGH.
9. Blend 1-2 x 15ml (1-2 tbsp) of cornflour with a little of the stock. The amount of cornflour depends on the thickness of the sauce required.
10. Pour back into the remaining 600ml (1pt) of reserved stock.
11. Cook for 3-4 minutes on HIGH. Stirring half way through the cooking time. Season to taste.
12. Add to the tripe and onions.
13. Reheat for 2-3 minutes on HIGH.

POULTRY
AND GAME

Roast Pheasant in Madeira Sauce

2 pheasants dressed
225g (8oz) streaky bacon
2 small onions
Madeira Wine Sauce
(see page 71)

1. Make Madeira wine sauce – see page 71.
2. Place bacon over pheasant breast to prevent the breast from drying. Place on low rack and cook for 10-15 minutes per 450g (1 lb) on **DUAL COOK** (on 160°C microwave **MED-LOW**). Baste the birds several times during cooking.
3. When the birds are cooked, place on serving dish.
4. Heat the Madeira sauce on **HIGH** for 1½-2 minutes and serve with the pheasants.

Crofters Pigeon Casserole

2 pigeons
2 rashers bacon
600ml (1pt) beef stock
2 x 15ml (2 tbsp) Madeira wine
(optional)
15g (½oz) cornflour
2 x 15ml (2 tbsp) water
2 x 15ml (2 tbsp) redcurrant jelly

1. Wrap pigeons in bacon. Place breast side down in a casserole dish.
2. Cover with stock, redcurrant jelly and Madeira wine. Cover with lid.
3. Cook for 50 minutes on **DUAL COOK** (on 160°C microwave **MED-LOW**). Turn over half way through cooking time.
4. Mix cornflour with water. Stir into pigeon stock. Cook on **HIGH** for 3-4 minutes.

Roast Venison

900g (2 lb) venison - well trussed

Marinade:
2 onions - sliced
2 carrots - sliced
1 clove garlic - chopped
1 stick celery - chopped
2 bay leaves
12 peppercorns
2 cloves
1 x 5ml (1 tsp) thyme
2 cups of red wine
4 x 15ml (4 tbsp) vegetable oil

1. Mix all the marinating ingredients together.
2. In a bowl place the venison. Pour over the marinade. Leave for 24 hours.
3. Remove the venison from the marinade.
4. Coat the venison well in cooking oil and place on low rack.
5. Cook for 13-15 minutes per 450g (1 lb) on **DUAL COOK** (on 160°C microwave **MED-LOW**).

1 medium duck
2 cloves garlic - peeled and cut into 4 wedges
150ml (¼pt) port wine
450ml (¾pt) beef stock
15ml (1 tbsp) redcurrant jelly
15ml (1 tbsp) corn flour
1 large tin black cherries - drained
salt and pepper

Duck with Black Cherry Sauce

1. Pierce the duck all over with a sharp knife. Insert the garlic pieces into the pierced breast skin.
2. Place breast side down on low wire rack and cook for 8-10 minutes per 450g (1 lb) on DUAL COOK (on 200°C microwave MED). Turn halfway through cooking time.
3. Stir port wine, beef stock and redcurrant jelly together. Blend a little of this with the cornflour then add remainder of the stock. Add drained cherries.
4. Skim fat off duck juices and add juices to wine/stock mixture. Heat for 5-6 minutes on HIGH, stirring 2-3 times during cooking. Season to taste.
5. Serve sauce with slices of duck.

4 chicken breasts
25g (1oz) butter
2 limes/lemons
white wine
2 x 5ml (2 tsp) cornflour
2 x 5ml (2 tsp) castor sugar to taste
2 spring onions - chopped
seasoning

Chicken in Lemon or Lime Sauce

1. Place the butter in a large dish and melt for 30 seconds on HIGH.
2. Cook the chicken breasts in butter for 7-9 minutes on HIGH. Re-arrange the chicken breasts half way through the cooking time. Remove the chicken breasts from the chicken juices.
3. Peel some of the rind from the limes/lemons and cut into very thin strips for garnish.
4. Place the juices from the limes/lemons into a measuring jug. Make the liquid up to 150ml (¼pt) with the white wine. Add spring onion.
5. Use a little of the juices from the white wine and lime, to make a smooth paste with the cornflour. Add to the remaining sauce.
6. Cook for 2½ minutes on HIGH, stirring half way through.
7. Add the strips of lime/lemon to the sauce, stir in the sugar - to taste. Season to taste.
8. Pour over the chicken breasts.

Turkey with Chestnut Stuffing

1. Place the chestnuts in a bowl with the breadcrumbs and sausagemeat and stir well to mix.
2. Add the butter, celery and onion with the seasoning and mix.
3. Add the beaten egg and bind together.
4. Stuff the neck of the turkey with the prepared stuffing.
5. Then coat the turkey breast with butter. Place on low rack.
6. Cook for 50-55 minutes on DUAL COOK (on 200°C microwave MED-HIGH). Turn over half way through cooking.

3.5kg (8 lb) turkey
440g (15½oz) can whole chestnuts, drained and finely chopped
100g (4oz) fresh white breadcrumbs
225g (8oz) pork sausagemeat
50g (2oz) butter - melted
1 stalk celery - chopped
1 medium onion - peeled and chopped
salt and pepper
1 egg beaten

Duck with Caramel and Orange Sauce

1. In a large dish place the shallots in the oil. Cook for 2 minutes on HIGH.
2. Pour on the stock, orange juice, castor sugar, white wine vinegar and seasoning. Place the duck in the dish, with the sauce. Place on low rack.
3. Cook for 35-45 minutes on DUAL COOK BAKE on 200°C. microwave MED-LOW).
4. Remove the duck pieces and place on a serving dish.
5. Skim off most of the fat from the sauce.
6. Strain the sauce.
7. Blend the cornflour with a little of the sauce, to form a smooth paste.
8. Add to the remaining sauce.
9. Cook for 2-3 minutes on HIGH or until thickened. Stir half way through the cooking time.
10. Accompany the duck pieces with the hot sauce - serving the sauce separately.

4 duck portions
1 x 5ml (1 tsp) oil
50g (2oz) shallots - chopped
25g (1oz) castor sugar
1 x 15ml (1 tbsp) white wine vinegar
175ml (6 fl oz) chicken stock
120ml (4 fl oz) orange juice
1 x 5ml (1 tsp) cornflour
seasoning

225g (8oz) cooked turkey - diced
1 red pepper - seeded and diced
50g (2oz) peas - cooked
1 small tin of sweetcorn
25g (1oz) plain flour
25g (1oz) margarine or butter
300ml (½pt) milk
salt and pepper

Turkey à la King

1. Melt the margarine or butter for 30 seconds on HIGH in a casserole dish. Stir in the flour.
2. Gradually add the milk. Cook for 3-4 minutes on HIGH. Stirring half way through the cooking time. Whisk until smooth. Season to taste
3. Add the remaining ingredients and cook for 2-3 minutes on HIGH, serve with rice.

4 chicken breasts
2 x 15ml (2 tbsp) liquid honey
1 x 5ml (1 tsp) mustard
½ x 5ml (½ tsp) tarragon
1 x 15ml (1 tbsp) tomato paste
150ml (¼pt) chicken stock
salt and black pepper
optional
1 x 5ml (1 tsp) cornflour - mixed to
smooth paste with water

Honeyed Chicken

1. Place the chicken breasts in a heat proof dish.
2. Mix all the other ingredients together and pour over the chicken. Place on low rack.
3. Cook for 20-25 minutes on DUAL COOK (on 200°C microwave MED-HIGH). Coat the chicken with the sauce several times during cooking.
4. Thicken with 1 tsp of cornflour 2 minutes before the end of the cooking.

Rabbit Casserole

1. Place vegetables in a large casserole dish.
2. Add the rabbit. Cover, completely with beef stock. Stir in the mixed herbs and seasoning.
3. Cover, and cook for 10 minutes on HIGH.
4. Stir and cook for 65-75 minutes on MED-LOW, or until the rabbit is tender.
5. Drain the sauce into a bowl.
6. Blend the cornflour with a little of the sauce. (The amount of cornflour required will depend on the quantity of sauce that is left after cooking) to form a smooth paste.
7. Pour back into the sauce. Cook for 4-5 minutes on HIGH, until the sauce has thickened. Stirring once during the cooking time.
8. Pour the thickened sauce over the rabbit. Garnish with chopped parsley.

1 rabbit - jointed
675g (1½ lb) vegetables - assorted
eg. carrots, onion, turnip
beef stock
2 x 15ml (2 tbsp) mixed herbs
1-2 x 15ml (1-2 tbsp) cornflour
seasoning

Chicken Satay

1. In a bowl mix all ingredients for the satay sauce (or use 1 bottle of satay sauce).
2. Add chicken cubes, coat thoroughly in sauce. Cover dish with microwave plastic wrap and place in fridge to marinate for 1-2 hours.
3. Skewer the chicken cubes, approximately four pieces on each skewer.
4. Place skewers on a baking sheet. Cook on DUAL COOK GRILL (microwave MEDIUM/GRILL) for 10 minutes.

4 chicken breasts - 2.5cm (1") cubes

Satay Sauce (or 1 bottle of satay sauce)
1 x 15ml (1 tbsp) soy sauce
1 x 15ml (1 tbsp) sunflower oil
2 x 5ml (2 tsp) ground coriander
2 x 5ml (2 tsp) ground cumin
1 x 5ml (1 tsp) ground turmeric
¼ x 5ml (¼ tsp) chilli powder
¼ x 5ml (¼ tsp) grated lemon rind and juice
1 x 5ml (1 tsp) dark brown sugar
100g (4oz) crunchy peanut butter
25g (1oz) desiccated coconut

4 large skewers

Sweet and Spicy Chicken

1. Cut the chicken into 7.5cm (3") strips. Mix egg white and 2 x 5ml (2tsp) cornflower together. Toss the chicken in the mixture and chill for 20 minutes.
2. Mix chicken stock, lemon juice, sugar, soy sauce, sherry, garlic, chopped pineapple and chilli powder together.
3. Mix a little of the liquid with the remaining 2 x 5ml (2 tsp) of cornflour to form a smooth paste then add to the sauce mixture. Cook for 3-4 minutes on HIGH or until the sauce has thickened. Stir once during cooking time.
4. Heat oil for 1 minute on HIGH in a large dish. Add the chicken and cook for 6-7 minutes, stirring twice, until chicken is white.
5. Pour the sauce over the chicken and cook for a further 2 minutes on HIGH. Toss the chicken then serve hot.

450g (1 lb) chicken breast
1 x size 3 egg white
2 x 5ml (2 tsp) cornflour
2 x 15ml (2 tbsp) oil
150ml (¼ pt) chicken stock
3 x 15ml (3 tbsp) fresh lemon juice
4 x 5ml (4 tsp) castor sugar
4 x 5ml (4 tsp) light soy sauce
4 x 5ml (4 tsp) dry sherry
1 clove garlic - crushed
½ x 5ml (½ tsp) chilli powder
2 x 5ml (2 tsp) cornflour
2 pineapple rings - chopped

340g (12oz) cooked turkey
1 medium onion - finely chopped
25g (1oz) margarine
1 medium cooking apple - peeled and
chopped
25g (1oz) sultanas
1-3 x 5ml (1-3 tsp) of curry powder or
paste (according to taste)
300ml (¹/2pt) chicken stock
1 clove garlic - crushed
¹/2 x 5ml (¹/2 tsp) ground ginger
2 bananas - sliced
seasoning

Turkey Curry

1. Melt the margarine in a large bowl for 30 seconds on HIGH. Add the onion, garlic and curry powder and cook for 3-4 minutes on HIGH.
2. Add the apple, sultanas, ginger and bananas. Stir, cover and cook for 3-4 minutes on HIGH.
3. Add the stock and turkey and cook for 15-20 minutes on MED-HIGH. Stir and cook for a further 5-6 minutes on HIGH.
4. Season to taste and serve with rice.

225g (8oz) mushrooms - sliced
1 medium onion - chopped
1 clove garlic - minced
4 x 15ml (4 tbsp) tomato purée
150ml (¹/4pt) water
150ml (¹/4pt) red wine
1 x 5ml (1 tsp) oregano
1 x 5ml (1 tsp) parsley (dried)
1 x 5ml (1 tsp) sugar
seasoning
4 chicken portions

Chicken Italienne

1. Cook mushrooms, garlic and onion in a large casserole for 4-5 minutes on HIGH.
2. Stir in remaining ingredients except chicken. Then add the chicken, coating with the sauce.
3. Cover and cook for 30-35 minutes on MED-HIGH. Stirring and coating the chicken twice during cooking time.
4. Stand for 10 minutes.

225g (8oz) puff pastry
1 cooked chicken
225g (8oz) flat mushrooms
25g (1oz) butter
salt and pepper
pinch of cayenne pepper

White sauce:

25g (1oz) butter
25g (1oz) plain flour
300ml (¹/2pt) stock
5 x 15ml (5 tbsp) cream
1 egg beaten
salt and pepper
25g (1oz) Parsley - chopped

Chicken and Mushroom Pie

1. Make the white sauce by melting the butter, cook for 30 seconds on HIGH. Then add the flour and blend well. Add the stock and seasoning. Mix well and cook for 3¹/2 minutes on HIGH.
2. Sauté the mushrooms in the butter cook for 2 minutes on HIGH. Then season with salt and pepper and add the spices.
3. Remove the meat from the chicken carcass in medium size pieces.
4. Add the parsley and cream to the white sauce. Arrange the chicken in layers in the pie dish with the mushrooms moistening well with the sauce.
5. Leave the chicken mixture until cold. Then cover with the rolled puff pastry. Glaze with an egg. Place on low rack.
6. Cook for 10-15 minutes on DUAL COOK (on 200°C microwave MEDIUM).

CHEESE AND EGG DISHES

Quiche Lorraine

200g (7oz) shortcrust pastry
1 onion - finely chopped
1 x 15ml (1 tbsp) oil
100g (4oz) bacon - chopped
75g (3oz) cheese -grated
2 eggs
300 ml (¹/₂pt) milk
1 x 5ml (1 tsp) mixed herbs
salt and pepper

1. Line a 17½cm (7'') flan ring with pastry.
2. Cover and sauté the onion in the oil for 3-4 minutes on HIGH.
3. Cook the chopped bacon for 2 minutes on HIGH.
4. Place the onion, bacon and grated cheese into flan case.
5. Beat together the eggs, milk, herbs and seasoning. Pour into flan case. Place on low rack.
6. Bake for 20-25 minutes on DUAL COOK BAKE (on 200°C microwave MED-LOW).

Stilton and Onion Quiche

200g (7oz) shortcrust pastry
1 onion - finely chopped
125g (5oz) blue stilton
1 x size 3 egg
150ml (¹/₄pt) milk
seasoning

1. Line a 17½cm (7'') flan dish with pastry. Place on low rack. Bake blind (with greaseproof paper and beans in the base) for 8 minutes on DUAL COOK BAKE (on 200°C microwave MED-LOW).
2. Place the sliced onion on the pastry base.
3. Mix the milk, egg, blue stilton and seasoning together. Pour over the onion.
4. Place on low rack and cook for 20-25 minutes on DUAL COOK BAKE (on 200°C microwave MED-LOW).

Calzone Pizza

1 packet bread mix (250-300g)
200g (7oz) ricotta cheese
150g (5oz) cooked spinach - chopped
100g (4oz) ham - chopped
100g (4oz) mushrooms - sliced
50g (2oz) mozzarella cheese - grated
salt and pepper
2 x 5ml (2 tsp) oregano
2 x 15ml (2 tbsp) milk

1. Make up bread mix according to instruction. Allow to prove.
2. Knock back dough and roll into a 12'' circle approx 5cm (0.5'') thick.
3. Mix ricotta cheese with oregano and seasoning.
4. Spread half of spinach over half of bread dough. Cover spinach with ricotta mixture, then ham and mushrooms then grated mozzarella. Cover with remaining spinach.
5. Brush edge of pizza with milk and then fold over to make a pastry shape. Press edges well and brush top with milk.
6. Bake on DUAL COOK (on 200°C microwave MED-LOW) for 30 minutes.

350g (12oz) shortcrust pastry
Filling:
2 large onions, finely sliced
225g (8oz) cheddar cheese, grated
25g (1oz) butter
1 x 15ml (1 tbsp) Worcestershire sauce
½ x 5ml (½ tsp) dried mustard
seasoning
1 egg beaten

Cheese and Onion Pie

1. Line a pie or flan dish with two thirds of the pastry. Roll out the rest for the lid.
2. Mix onions and cheese, mustard and sauce.
3. Put filling into pastry case, dot with butter.
4. Place lid on top of pie press to seal. Glaze with beaten egg. Make a slit to let out steam. Place on low rack.
5. Bake for 18-22 minutes on DUAL COOK BAKE (on 200°C microwave MED-LOW).

150ml (¼pt) water
50g (2oz) butter or margarine
70g (2½oz) plain flour
punch of salt
2 x size 3 eggs - lightly beaten
1 x 5ml (1 tsp) mixed herbs
25g (oz) butter
1 small onion - finely chopped
125g (5oz) mushrooms - sliced
25g (1oz) plain flour
1 chicken stock cube
8 x 15ml (8 tbsp) boiling water
8 x 15ml (8 tbsp) single cream
5ml (1 tsp) grainy mustard
225g (8oz) chopped ham
100g (4oz) grated cheese
1 medium tomato - sliced

Herby Gougere

1. Preheat oven to 200°C.
2. Heat water and butter for 2-3 minutes on HIGH.
3. Add flour and salt, beat well. Cook for 1 minute on HIGH.
4. Gradually add eggs and beat well.
5. Spoon or pipe into a ring on a greased baking sheet.
6. Place butter, onion, mushrooms into a large bowl. Heat for 2-3 minutes on HIGH. Stir in flour.
7. Mix stock cube with boiling water and stir into the mixture with cream and mustard. Cook for 2-3 minutes on HIGH until mixture has thickened.
8. Stir in ham and cheese and spoon into centre of choux ring. Decorate with sliced tomato.
9. Cook in preheated oven on low rack for 25-30 minutes at CONVECTION 200°C until golden.

60g (2½oz) margarine
60g (2½oz) plain flour
½ x 5ml (½ tsp) salt
⅛ x 5ml (⅛ tsp) cayenne pepper
375ml (13 fl oz) milk
250g (9oz) grated cheese
6 x size 3 eggs - separated

Cheese Soufflé

1. Place margarine in a large bowl. Cook for 1 minute on HIGH until melted. Blend in flour, salt and cayenne pepper. Gradually stir in milk and cook on MED-HIGH until slightly thickened, about 6-7 minutes, stirring every 2 minutes. Add cheese, cook for 2 minutes on MED-HIGH, stir to blend.
2. Beat egg yolks. Stir a small amount of hot sauce gradually into the egg yolks, return to sauce, blending well. Cool slightly.
3. Beat egg whites until soft peaks form. With spatula fold egg whites into cheese sauce, half at a time just until blended. Pour into a greased 2 litre (4pt) soufflé dish. Place on low rack.
4. Bake for 18-22 minutes on DUAL COOK (on 200°C microwave LOW) until top is puffed and golden and centre is set. Serve immediately.

Pizza

1. Make pizza base as instructed on the packet to make 10'' pizza.
2. Place on 25cm pizza tray (or round metal tray).
3. Mix the tomato purée, tomatoes, onions, garlic, marjoram, mustard powder and dried oregano together.
4. Spread onto pizza dough.
5. Sprinkle over the grated cheddar cheese.
6. Place black olives and capers on top.
7. Season to taste. Place metal pizza tray on the low metal rack. Cover and cook for 25 minutes on DUAL COOK (on 200°C microwave MED-LOW).

1 pizza dough mix (makes approximately 10" pizza)
2 x 15ml (2 tbsp) tomato purée
198g (7oz) tin chopped tomatoes
1 large onion - chopped
2 cloves garlic - chopped
2 x 5ml (2 tsp) dried marjoram
1/2 x 5ml (1/2 tsp) mustard powder
1/2 x 5ml (1/2 tsp) dried oregano
100g (4oz) cheddar cheese - grated
100g (4oz) black olives - stoned
1 x 15ml (1 tbsp) capers
salt and pepper

Puffy Omelette

1. Place margarine in a 23cm (9") non-metallic pie plate. Cook for 30-45 seconds on HIGH until melted. Separate eggs, placing egg whites in a large mixing bowl and egg yolks in a medium bowl. Blend remaining ingredients into egg yolks. Beat whites with electric mixer until stiff but not dry.
2. Fold egg yolk mixture into beaten egg whites with spatula. Pour into plate.
3. Cook on MEDIUM until centre is set, 4-6 minutes.

Cheese Omelette Variation: Sprinkle 225g (8oz) grated cheese over cooked omelette. Cook for 30 seconds - 1 minute on MED-HIGH until cheese melts.

1 x 15ml (1 tbsp) margarine or butter
4 eggs
75ml (1/8pt) milk
1/4 x 5ml (1/4 tsp) baking powder
1/4 x 5ml (1/4 tsp) salt
dash of pepper

Omelette

1. Beat the eggs in a medium sized bowl with milk or water, salt and pepper until well mixed.
2. Melt the butter in a 25cm (10") non-metallic pie dish for 30 seconds, coat the dish completely with butter.
3. Pour the egg mixture into the pie dish. Cover tightly with microwave plastic wrap.
4. Cook for 2 minutes on HIGH.
5. With a fork move the cooked mixture towards the centre.
6. Cook covered for 1½ minutes on HIGH.
7. Let stand covered for at least 1½ minutes.
8. Loosen the omelette from the plate, fold in half and place on a serving dish.

Variations:

Cheese Omelette - sprinkle with 50g (2oz) grated cheese after step 6, cover and heat for an additional 30 seconds.

Bacon Omelette - cook bacon before preparing omelette, add bacon to egg mixture during step 1.

4 x size 3 eggs
3 x 15ml (3 tbsp) milk or water
1/4 x 5ml (1/4 tsp) salt
pepper to taste
1 x 15ml (1 tbsp) butter or margarine

SAUCES

Orange Sauce

200ml (⅓pt) orange juice
grated orange (optional)
2 x 5ml (2 tsp) castor sugar
15g (½oz) cornflour
100ml (3 fl oz) water

In a jug mix sugar and cornflour to a smooth paste with a little of the orange juice. Then add remainder of orange juice and water - and orange rind if used. Cook for 1½ minutes on HIGH, stirring once.

Bread Sauce

1 peeled onion, studded with cloves
4 peppercorns
pinch nutmeg
250ml (½pt) milk
25g (1oz) butter or margarine
75g (3oz) breadcrumbs
6 x 15ml (6 tbsp) milk

Put studded onion, peppercorns, nutmeg and milk into a jug. Heat on HIGH for 3 minutes. Leave to infuse for 5 minutes. Strain milk liquor over breadcrumbs and butter or margarine. Cook for 3-4 minutes on HIGH. Stir in remaining 6 tbsp milk.

Bechamel Sauce

300ml (½pt) milk
1 small onion - sliced
½ stick celery -chopped
1 small carrot - sliced
2 cloves
6 white peppercorns
25g (1oz) margarine or butter
25g (1oz) plain flour
seasoning

1. Put milk, onion, carrot, celery, cloves and peppercorns into a jug. Cook for 3-4 minutes on MEDIUM.
2. Cover and leave to infuse for 30 minutes. Strain and reserve liquor.
3. Melt butter or margarine for 30 seconds on HIGH. Stir in flour. Gradually add strained milk.
4. Cook for 3-3½ minutes on HIGH, whisking once.
5. Season to taste.

Confectioners Custard

300ml (½pt) milk
2 x size 3 egg yolks
25g (1oz) cornflour
25g (1oz) castor sugar
a few drops of vanilla essence

1. Blend the cornflour with a little of the milk until it forms a smooth paste.
2. In a bowl, mix the egg yolks and castor sugar. Add the milk, cornflour mixture and the vanilla essence. Stir well.
3. Cook for 7-8 minutes on MEDIUM whisking every 2 minutes, until the mixture has thickened.

Apple Sauce

1 large cooking apple - peeled and chopped

Place chopped apple in a covered basin. Cook for 3-3½ minutes on HIGH. Mash with a fork, add a little water if necessary.

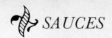

45g (1½oz) butter/margarine
25g (1oz) curry powder
45g (1½oz) plain flour
1 onion - finely chopped
1 x 15ml (1 tbsp) lemon juice
1 x 5ml (1 tsp) mango chutney
  (optional)
600ml (1pt) milk
300ml (½pt) chicken or vegetable stock
salt and pepper to taste

Curry Sauce

1. Melt butter for 30 seconds on HIGH in a large microwaveable bowl.
2. Add the curry powder and onion to the butter, stir well, cook for 1 minute on HIGH.
3. Stir in the flour, milk, stock, chutney, lemon juice. Cook for 5-6 minutes on HIGH until thickened. Season to taste.

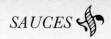

Custard Sauce

1 x 15ml (1 tbsp) custard powder
300ml (½pt) milk
1 x 15ml (1 tbsp) sugar

1. Combine custard powder with milk in a large jug. Heat, uncovered for 3-3½ minutes on HIGH.
2. When thickened, whisk in sugar until dissolved.

Barbecue Sauce

1 medium onion - chopped
1 clove garlic - crushed
1 x 15ml (1 tbsp) vegetable oil
300ml (½pt) tomato sauce
50g (2oz) brown sugar
2 x 15ml (2 tbsp) cider vinegar
¼ x 5ml (¼ tsp) dry mustard
¼ x 5ml (¼ tsp) salt
4 to 6 drops tabasco sauce

1. Combine onion, garlic and oil in a 2 litre (4pt) casserole dish. Cover and cook on HIGH until onion is tender, 2½-4½ minutes, stirring once.
2. Stir in remaining ingredients. Microwave on HIGH until hot, 3-4 minutes. Reduce power to MED-HIGH. Microwave until flavours blend, 5-6 minutes. Serve over meat.

Basic White Sauce

25g (1oz) butter or margarine
25g (1oz) plain flour
300ml (½pt) milk
salt and pepper

1. Place butter or margarine in a bowl or jug and heat for 30 seconds on HIGH until melted.
2. Stir in flour and blend in milk.
3. Heat for 3-3½ minutes on HIGH until thickened. Whisk until smooth. Season.

Variations:

Cheese Sauce: Stir in 75g (3oz) grated cheese and 1 x 5ml (1 tsp) made mustard into finished sauce.

Mushroom Sauce: Stir in 50g-100g (2-4oz) lightly cooked thinly sliced mushrooms into finished sauce.

Parsley Sauce: Stir in 1-2 x 15ml (1-2 tbsp) chopped parsley into finished sauce.

Onion Sauce: Stir in 1 large boiled and finely chopped onion into finished sauce.

Sweet White Sauce: Omit salt and pepper from basic sauce, stir in sugar to taste.

Marmalade or Jam Sauce

1 x 15ml (1 tbsp) marmalade or jam
1 x 5ml (1 tsp) castor sugar
150ml (¼pt) water
½ x 5ml (½ tsp) cornflour
a little lemon juice

1. Put marmalade or jam, sugar, and water in a glass bowl or jug and heat for 1½ minutes on HIGH until boiling.
2. Mix cornflour with a little cold water and add to jam mixture. Heat on HIGH until boiling and clear. Add lemon juice.

Rich Brown Sauce

25g (1oz) margarine
1 chopped onion
1 chopped carrot
1 stick celery, chopped
1 x 5ml (1 tsp) gravy browning
25g (1oz) plain flour
300ml (½pt) beef stock
seasoning

In a bowl melt margarine for 30 seconds on HIGH. Add chopped vegetables and cook on HIGH for 5 minutes. Stir in gravy browning and flour. Cook on HIGH for 1 minute. Gradually stir in the stock. Cook for 3-3½ minutes on HIGH, stirring once. Strain the sauce and season to taste.

Variation)

Madeira wine sauce: Add 50ml (2 fl oz) Madeira wine at end of cooking.

VEGETABLE DISHES

Stuffed Peppers

1. Cut the tops off the two peppers. Scoop out the seeds and core.
2. Place on a dish, cover and cook for 2 minutes on HIGH.
3. Place rice in a dish, dissolve the chicken stock cube in the hot water then pour over the rice. Add the onion and bay leaf. Stir, cover and cook for 7-8 minutes on HIGH.
4. Stir the rice, add the peas and sweetcorn then cover and cook for a further 2 minutes - or until all the liquid is absorbed by the rice. Remove the bay leaf.
5. Add the chopped ham and sultanas. Season to taste.
6. Fill the peppers with the rice filling.
7. Before serving, reheat peppers for 1-2 minutes on HIGH.

2 large red peppers
50g (2oz) long grain rice
1 chicken stock cube
200ml (1/3pt) water
1 onion - peeled and chopped
1 bay leaf
25g (1oz) peas
25g (1oz) sweetcorn
50g (2oz) ham - chopped
25g (1oz) sultanas (optional)
salt and pepper

Parsnips in Honey

1. Prepare parsnips. Peel, cut into quarters and place in a dish with the water.
2. Pour over the honey.
3. Cook covered for 7-8 minutes on HIGH.

450g (1 lb) parsnips
2 x 15ml (2 tbsp) water
2 x 5ml (2 tsp) clear honey

Ratatouille

1. Layer the vegetables in a large casserole dish. Pour over the tinned tomatoes. Add the garlic clove. Cover the dish with microwave plastic wrap.
2. Cook for 14-16 minutes on MED-HIGH, until vegetables are tender. Season to taste. Stand for 5 minutes before serving.

1 aubergine - sliced
1 medium chopped onion
1 large sliced courgette
1 x 400g (14oz) tin tomatoes
50g (2oz) whole green beans
1 clove garlic - crushed
1/2 red pepper deseeded and sliced
1/2 green pepper deseeded and sliced
seasoning

Cauliflower Cheese

1. Remove thick stalk from centre of cauliflower, but keep whole.
2. Place in a dish with 2 x 15ml (2 tbsp) water. Cover with microwave plastic wrap.
3. Cook for 9-14 minutes on MED-HIGH, depending on size of cauliflower.
4. Make white sauce - see page 71.
5. Add 50g (2oz) of the grated cheese and pour over cauliflower.
6. Sprinkle remaining cheese and breadcrumbs over the top and place on high rack. Grill until crispy and golden brown on top.

1 medium cauliflower
300ml (1/2pt) white sauce (see page 71)
125g (5oz) grated cheese
15g (1/2 oz) breadcrumbs

450g (1 lb) swede
450g (1 lb) carrots
10 x 15ml (10 tbsp) water
50g (2oz) butter
salt and pepper

Puréed Swede and Carrots

1. Peel and chop the swede and carrots. Cut into even sized pieces.
2. In one bowl place the cubed swede. Add 5 x 15ml (5 tbsp) of water. Cover and cook for 8-9 minutes on HIGH until soft.
3. In a bowl place the cubed carrots. Add the 5 x 15ml (5 tbsp) of water. Cover and cook for 8-9 minutes on HIGH until soft.
4. Mash the cooked swede with 25g (1oz) of the butter. Place into ramekin dishes. Leave for about 10-15 minutes or until cool.
5. Mash the cooked carrot with 25g (1oz) of the butter. Place into ramekin dishes. Leave for about 10-15 minutes or until cool.
6. Turn out the swede and carrot from the moulds.
7. Reheat for 2-3 minutes on HIGH.

400g (14oz) carrots - sliced
2 x 15ml (2 tbsp) orange juice
2 x 15ml (2 tbsp) brown sugar
12.5g (½oz) butter
Seasoning

Sweet Carrots

Place all ingredients together in a large bowl. Cover and cook for 7-9 minutes on HIGH. Stir 2 or 3 times throughout cooking.

450g (1 lb) broccoli
2 x 15ml (2 tbsp) water

Lemon sauce:
100ml (4 fl oz) water
50ml (2 fl oz) lemon juice
1 x 5ml (1 tsp) cornflour

Broccoli in Lemon Sauce

1. Place broccoli in a dish with 2 x 15ml (2 tbsp) water.
2. Cook for 8-9 minutes on HIGH in a covered dish.
3. Mix the cornflour with a little of the water to make a smooth paste, then mix with remaining water and lemon juice.
4. Cook sauce for 2½ minutes on HIGH, stirring once.
5. Drain broccoli and pour lemon sauce over.

2 large baking potatoes
50g (2oz) cheese - finely grated
50g (2oz) butter
50g (2oz) ham - chopped
2 x 5ml (2 tsp) wholegrain mustard
salt and pepper

Stuffed Potato Skins

1. Wrap potatoes in kitchen paper and cook for 14-17 minutes on microwave HIGH until cooked. Allow to stand for 5 minutes.
2. Cut each potato into quarters. Scoop out potato from skins. Mash potato with cheese, butter, ham, wholegrain mustard and seasoning.
3. Put filling into skins. Place on heatproof plate.
4. Cook on high rack for 7-11 minutes on DUAL COOK GRILL (microwave LOW/GRILL) until golden.

50g (2oz) butter
225g (8oz) peeled carrots - cut into
thin matchsticks
15ml (1 tbsp) finely chopped celery tops

Glazed Carrots

1. Melt butter for 1-2 minutes on microwave HIGH.
2. Add carrots, cover and cook for 4-4½ minutes on microwave HIGH.
3. Stir in chopped celery tops and leave to stand covered for 5 minutes.

Mange Tout and Baby Sweetcorn

225g (8oz) mange tout
225g (8oz) baby sweetcorn
25g (1oz) butter
seasoning

1. Melt butter for 1 minute on HIGH in a bowl.
2. Add sweetcorn and cook covered for 2 minutes on HIGH.
3. Add mange tout. Cook covered for 3-4 minutes on HIGH. Season to taste.

Courgettes Provençal

2 sliced courgettes
1 chopped onion
400g (14oz) tinned tomatoes - drained and chopped
1 clove of garlic - crushed
1 x 15ml (1 tbsp) oil
1 x 15ml (1 tbsp) oregano

1. Cook onion and garlic in oil 1 minute on HIGH in a dish.
2. Add tomatoes and oregano.
3. Cover and cook for 3 minutes on HIGH.
4. Add courgettes and cook for 4-5 minutes on HIGH.

Brussels Sprouts with Almonds

450g (1 lb) brussels sprouts - peeled
2 x 15ml (2 tbsp) water
50g (2oz) flaked almonds
50g (2oz) butter
seasoning

1. Cook sprouts with water in a covered dish for 9-10 minutes on HIGH.
2. Place almonds and butter in a dish and cook for 1½ minutes on HIGH.
3. Pour almonds and butter over sprouts and season to taste.

CEREALS
AND GRAINS

Lasagne

1. Place mince, tomatoes, onion, stock, herbs and pepper into a large bowl. Cover and cook for 20-25 minutes on MEDIUM.
2. Melt butter for 45 seconds on HIGH in a bowl. Add flour and mix well. Cook for 1 minute on HIGH.
3. Gradually beat in milk and cook for 6 minutes on HIGH beating once half way through cooking. Add 50g (2oz) grated cheese.
4. In a casserole dish layer meat, lasagne and cheese sauce alternately, making two layers of each finishing off with grated cheese.
5. Sprinkle top with grated cheese. Place on low rack.
6. Cook for 10-15 minutes on DUAL COOK (on 200°C microwave LOW).

450g (1 lb) minced beef
1 x 400g (14oz) can chopped tomatoes
150ml (¼pt) stock
1 x 15ml (1 tbsp) mixed herbs
½ green pepper - chopped
1 onion - chopped
175g (6oz) lasagne - pre-cooked
50g (2oz) butter
50g (2oz) flour
600ml (1pt) milk
75g (3oz) cheddar cheese - grated

Tagliatelle with Ham and Cream Sauce

1. Melt the butter for 30 seconds on HIGH in a bowl.
2. Add the chopped ham and red pepper cook for 1 minute on HIGH. Stir in the flour.
3. Gradually add the cream and milk and chives.
4. Cook for 3-3½ minutes on HIGH, stirring once.
5. Season to taste. Serve with cooked tagliatelle.
N.B.
To cook tagliatelle place in hot bowl with twice the volume of hot water. Cook for 8-12 minutes on HIGH.

225g (8oz) tagliatelle - cooked
25g (1oz) butter
100g (4oz) ham - chopped
25g (1oz) flour
150ml (¼pt) double cream
150ml (¼pt) milk
1 small red pepper - chopped
1 x 15ml (1 tbsp) chives - chopped
seasoning to taste

Neapolitan Sauce

1. Place onion, garlic, celery and margarine in a large dish. Cook for 3 minutes on HIGH.
2. Add tomatoes, wine, oregano, mushrooms and seasoning.
3. Cover and cook for 10-12 minutes on HIGH.

1 large onion - chopped
1 clove garlic - crushed
2 sticks celery - chopped
25g (1oz) margarine
400g (14oz) tin tomatoes - chopped
150ml (¼pt) red wine
2 x 5ml (2 tsp) oregano
100g (4oz) mushrooms - chopped
seasoning

Beef Risotto

1. In a casserole dish place the oil, chopped onion, celery, green pepper, red pepper and sliced beef fillet. Cook for 5 minutes on HIGH. Stir halfway through cooking time.
2. Add the cayenne pepper, ground cumin, lemon juice and rind, sweetcorn, peas, long grain rice and beef stock. Season.
3. Stir well, cover and cook for 12-15 minutes on HIGH until rice is tender.

2 x 15ml (2 tbsp) vegetable oil
1 small onion - peeled and chopped
1 stick celery - chopped
1 small green pepper - seeded and sliced
1 small red pepper - seeded and sliced
175g (6oz) beef fillet - thinly sliced
    into 5cm (2") strips
½ x 5ml (½ tsp) cayenne pepper
1 x 5ml (1 tsp) ground cumin
juice and grated rind of 1 lemon
50g (2oz) sweetcorn
50g (2oz) peas
225g (8oz) long grain rice - easy cook
600ml (1pt) beef stock
salt and pepper

Fried Rice

1. Combine onion and margarine or butter in a 2 litre (3½pt) casserole dish. Cook on HIGH until onion is tender, for 3 minutes. Set aside.
2. Stir stock cubes into hot water until dissolved. Add stock, rice and shallots to casserole, cover, cook on HIGH until liquid is absorbed, 8-12 minutes.
3. Stir in eggs and soy sauce. Cook, uncovered, on HIGH until eggs are set, 2-4 minutes, stir several times during cooking. Fluff with a fork before serving. Season to taste.

2 x 15ml (2 tbsp) chopped onion
1 x 15ml (1 tbsp) margarine or butter
2 chicken stock cubes
600ml (1pt) hot water
450g (1 lb) quick cook long grain rice
2 x 15ml (2 tbsp) finely chopped
shallots or spring onions
3 x size 2 eggs - beaten
1 x 15ml (1 tbsp) plus 2 x 15ml
2 x 15ml (2 tbsp) soy sauce
seasoning

Rice Pilaf

1. Combine onion, celery, green pepper and margarine or butter in a 1 litre (1¾pt) casserole dish. Cook on HIGH until vegetables are tender-crisp, 3-5 minutes. Stir in remaining ingredients. Cover.
2. Cook for 5 minutes on HIGH. Reduce power to MEDIUM. Cook until liquid is absorbed, 12-14 minutes. Let stand, covered, 5 minutes. Fluff with fork before serving.

2 x 15ml (2 tbsp) chopped onion
2 x 15ml (2 tbsp) chopped celery
2 x 15ml (2 tbsp) chopped green pepper
2 x 15ml (2 tbsp) margarine or butter
300ml (½pt) hot water
100g (4oz) sliced mushrooms
75g (3oz) uncooked long grain rice
1 chicken stock cube crumbled
seasoning

Macaroni Cheese

1. In a bowl place the bacon and onion.
2. Cook for 3 minutes on HIGH. Add the flour and milk. Mix thoroughly. Add seasoning and ¾ of the grated cheese. Stir well add pre-cooked macaroni.
3. Place the mixture into a casserole dish. Sprinkle the remaining cheese over the top. Place on low rack.
4. Cook for 10-15 minutes on DUAL COOK BAKE (on 200°C microwave MED-LOW), or until the surface is golden brown.

175g (6oz) cooked macaroni
100g (4oz) bacon - chopped
1 onion - chopped
37g (1½ oz) flour
600ml (1pt) milk
175g (6oz) cheddar cheese - grated
salt and pepper

DESSERTS

Lemon Meringue Pie

175g (6oz) shortcrust pastry
3 x 15ml (3 tbsp) cornflour
300ml (½pt) water
2 lemons, juice and grated rind
75g (3oz) castor sugar
25g (1oz) butter
3 x size 3 eggs, separated
175g (6oz) castor sugar

1. Line a 18cm (7'') flan dish with pastry. Bake blind for 10-15 minutes on low rack on DUAL COOK BAKE (on 200°C microwave MED-LOW).
2. Mix the cornflour with the water, add lemon juice, rind and 75g (3oz) sugar. Cook for 3-3½ minutes on HIGH, stirring once until it thickens. Stir well.
3. Add butter and egg yolks. Beat well. Pour into flan case.
4. Whisk egg whites until stiff. Whisk in half the sugar, then fold in the rest.
5. Pipe or spoon onto filling. Cook on CONVECTION 180°C for 10-15 minutes, until golden.

Coffee Renoir

Choux pastry:
150ml (¼pt) water
50g (2oz) margarine or butter
70g (2½oz) plain flour
pinch of salt
2 x size 3 eggs - lightly beaten

Filling - custard:
300ml (½pt) milk
2 x size 3 egg yolks
25g (1oz) cornflour
25g (1oz) castor sugar
A few drops of vanilla essence

Filling - cream:
150ml (¼pt) whipping cream
1 x 5ml (1 tsp) icing sugar

Icing:
100g (4oz) icing sugar - sieved
3 x 5ml (3 tsp) instant coffee
2-3 x 5ml (2-3 tsp) water

1. Heat the water and margarine or butter in a bowl for 2 minutes on HIGH, until boiling.
2. Quickly add the flour and salt, beat well. Cook for 1 minute on HIGH.
3. Pre-heat the oven to 200°C.
4. Gradually add the eggs and beat well.
5. Lightly grease the turntable, and pipe the choux pastry in a 18cm (7'') ring.
6. Sprinkle a few drops of water around the turntable. Cook in a pre-heated oven on 200°C for 15-20 minutes. Then lower the setting to 160°C for 10-15 minutes - to dry the centre of the pastry ring.
7. Take the choux ring out of the oven. Slice the ring in half, lengthways. Scrape all the dough from the bottom half of the choux ring.
8. Place the top part of the choux ring back onto a turntable with cut side uppermost. Cook again for 10-15 minutes on 160°C, until the centre of the choux ring has crisped up.
9. Make the custard filling by blending the cornflour with half of the milk. In a bowl mix the egg yolks and castor sugar. Add the milk, cornflour mixture and the vanilla essence. Stir well.
10. Cook for 7 minutes on MEDIUM whisking every 2 minutes, until the mixture has thickened. Leave to cool.
11. Whisk the cream with the icing sugar, until stiff.
12. Mix the coffee icing by dissolving the coffee in hot water. Sieve the icing sugar, mix to form a stiff icing.
13. Spread the custard on the base of the choux ring. Over the top of the custard spread the cream. Place the top choux ring over the cream, and spread the coffee icing on the top.

N.B. Make sure the choux ring is cooked when removed from the oven, otherwise it may collapse on cooling.

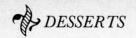

100g (4oz) castor sugar
4 x size 3 eggs - separated
100g (4oz) plain chocolate, broken into pieces
25g (1oz) icing sugar - sifted
300ml (½pt) double cream, whipped

Chocolate Roulade

1. Preheated oven to 200°C.
2. Grease and line a swiss role tin.
3. Beat together castor sugar and egg yolks until thick, pale and creamy. Beat egg whites until stiff and forms peaks.
4. Place chocolate pieces into microwaveable dish and heat for 2½-3½ minutes on HIGH until melted.
5. Stir melted chocolate into egg yolk and sugar. Fold in egg whites.
6. Pour chocolate mixture into prepared tin. Place tin on low rack and cook for 15-18 minutes on CONVECTION 200°C.
7. When cooked, turn Roulade onto a sheet of greaseproof paper, which is dusted with icing sugar. Trim edges of Roulade with sharp knife.
8. Spread double cream over Roulade and roll up.
   (Roulade will crack)

300ml (½pt) milk
2 eggs, beaten and strained
50g (2oz) castor sugar
225g (8oz) fruit - cooked or tinned
2 x 15ml (2 tbsp) soft brown sugar

Fruit Brûlée

1. Pour milk into a bowl and warm through for 2 minutes on HIGH.
2. Place fruit in a 1200ml (2pt) straight sided dish.
3. Beat eggs and sugar into milk, and pour over fruit.
4. Cover and cook for 7-8 minutes on MEDIUM, until lightly set.
5. Uncover and sprinkle the surface with brown sugar. Place on high rack. Grill until sugar melts and turns golden brown. Approx. 8-10 minutes.

Pastry:
200g (7oz) plain flour
1 x 15ml (1 tbsp) castor sugar
½ x 5ml (½ tsp) salt
50g (2oz) lard
50g (2oz) margarine
3-4 x 15ml (3-4 tbsp) milk - to mix

Filling:
450g (16oz) golden syrup
175g (6oz) fresh breadcrumbs

Treacle Tart

1. To make pastry mix together flour, castor sugar and salt. Rub in lard and margarine to resemble fine breadcrumbs. Mix to a stiff dough with milk.
2. Line a greased 21.5cm (8.5″) pie dish with pastry. Lightly prick the pastry with a fork. Bake blind for 3½-4 minutes on HIGH.
3. In a non-metallic bowl, mix golden syrup and breadcrumbs together. Cook for 2-3 minutes on HIGH. Add mixture to pastry case and cook for 3-3½ minutes on HIGH.

Magic Lemon Pudding

Grated rind and juice of 1 lemon
50g (2oz) butter
100g (4oz) castor sugar
2 x size 3 eggs - separated
50g (2oz) self raising flour
300ml (½pt) milk

1. Beat lemon rind, butter and castor sugar together until light and fluffy. Add the egg yolks and self raising flour. Beat well.
2. Stir in the milk and lemon juice.
3. Whisk egg whites until stiff, fold into lemon mixture.
4. Pour mixture into microwaveable loaf dish. Stand in a shallow dish of water and cook on low rack for 25-30 minutes on DUAL COOK (on 200°C microwave LOW).

*This pudding gives a light sponge with a creamy sauce below.

Summer Pudding

8 slices of medium sliced bread, crusts removed
100g (4oz) castor sugar
900g (2 lb) soft summer fruits (eg. raspberries, strawberries, blackcurrants, redcurrants, blackberries, etc)
5 x 15ml (5 tbsp) water

1. Line a 2pt pudding basin with the bread slices, reserving enough for a lid.
2. Place the castor sugar and 5 tablespoons of water into a large microwaveable bowl. Heat for 2 minutes on HIGH. Add fruit and cook for 4-5 minutes on HIGH.
3. Using a slotted spoon, place fruit into the lined dish. Add 60ml (4 tablespoons) of fruit juice.
4. Cover fruit with remaining bread and pour over 2 tablespoons of juice. (Reserve remaining juice).
5. Cover pudding with a saucer and place a small weight on top. leave to stand in fridge overnight.
6. Pour remaining juice over pudding if there are still areas of uncoloured bread. Turn out onto serving plate.

Cherry Mallow Crunch

75g (3oz) butter
175g (6oz) half coated chocolate biscuits - crushed
15g (½oz) gelatine - one sachet
45ml (3 tbsp) cold water
225g (8oz) pink marshmallows - approx 30
300ml (½pt) whole milk
50g (2oz) chopped glacé cherries
150ml (¼pt) double cream

1. Place butter in a large heatproof bowl. Heat for 1-2 minutes on HIGH until melted.
2. Mix the biscuits into the melted butter. Press into the base of a loose bottomed 18cm (7'') cake tin. Place into the refrigerator to set.
3. In a small heatproof bowl place gelatine and water, heat for 30-45 seconds on HIGH, until gelatine is melted. Stir well and allow to cool.
4. Place the marshmallows and milk into a large heatproof bowl and heat for 2-3 minutes on HIGH until marshmallows are melted. Whisk the mixture together with the gelatine and glace cherries. Cool until almost set, whisking every 10 minutes.
5. Whip the cream until it forms soft peaks, and fold into the marshmallow mixture.
6. Pour into prepared tin and chill until set (approx 2-3 hours).
7. Remove from tin. Decorate with cream and cherries if desired.

Caramel:

6 x 15ml (6 tbsp) castor sugar
2 x 15ml (2 tbsp) hot water

Custard:

2 x eggs size 3
1½ x 15ml (1½ tbsp) castor sugar
450ml (¾pt) milk

Crême Caramel

1. Mix the sugar and water for caramel in a pudding basin.
2. Cook for 4-5 minutes on HIGH, or until the caramel turns light golden brown.
3. Pour into the base of 4 ramekin dishes. Set aside.
4. Lightly whisk together eggs and sugar, stir in the milk.
5. Pour the mixture into the ramekin dishes. Place ramekins in a large dish.
6. Pour almost boiling water into the dish to reach the level of the custard.
7. Cook for 7-8 minutes on HIGH. Chill before turning out and serving.

400g (14oz) pineapple chunks
150g (5oz) butter
150g (5oz) demerara sugar
2 x size 3 eggs
1 x 15ml (1 tbsp) milk
100g (4oz) self raising flour
1 x 5ml (1 tsp) baking powder
2 x 5ml (2 tsp) ground ginger

Pineapple Ginger Sponge

1. In a heat proof dish place 25g (1oz) of the butter and 40g (1½oz) of the sugar. Cook on HIGH 1-1½ minutes to caramelise.
2. Drain pineapple and arrange two thirds in the bottom of the dish with the caramel in.
3. Beat the rest of the butter and sugar together, gradually beat in the eggs, mix in the flour, ginger and baking powder, then add the milk and the remaining pineapple (chop roughly and pat dry with kitchen paper).
4. Spoon the mixture into the dish. Cook for 6 minutes on HIGH. Allow to stand for 8-10 minutes.

Sussex Pond Pudding

350g (12oz) self raising flour
175g (6oz) shredded suet
175ml (6 fl oz) cold water
100g (4oz) butter
100g (4oz) light brown sugar
100g (4oz) sultanas
1 large lemon

1. Line a 1200ml (2pt) pudding basin with microwave plastic wrap.
2. Mix the flour and suet together and bind together with enough cold water to make a firm dough.
3. Roll out ¾ of the pastry and line the basin.
4. Cream the butter and sugar, and stir in the sultanas.
5. Prick the lemon all over with a fork.
6. Spoon a little of the sultana mixture into the basin. Stand the lemon upright in the centre and pack the remaining mixture around the lemon.
7. Roll out the remaining pastry to make a lid. Press the edges together and seal with water.
8. Cover loosely with dampened microwave plastic wrap.
9. Cook for 5-6 minutes on HIGH, standing on the low metal rack on the turntable.

Sultana Suet Pudding

100g (4oz) self raising flour
50g (2oz) shredded suet
50g (2oz) castor sugar
50g (2oz) sultanas
1 x size 3 egg - beaten
6 x 15ml (6 tbsp) milk
syrup

1. Place all dry ingredients into a bowl and mix well.
2. Add the egg and sufficient milk to make a very soft dough.
3. Place mixture into a pudding dish 600ml (1pt) and cover loosely with microwave plastic wrap.
4. Cook for 3-4 minutes on HIGH.
5. Leave to stand then turn out and pour syrup over.

Bread and Butter Pudding

6 thin slices bread
50g (2oz) butter
50g (2oz) sultanas
50g (2oz) castor sugar
300ml (½pt) milk
25g (1oz) candied peel

1. Remove crusts from the bread and spread slices thickly with butter. Cut into squares or fingers.
2. Place half of the bread, buttered side uppermost in a 1 litre (1¾pt) buttered dish. Sprinkle with fruit, peel, and half the sugar.
3. Top with remaining bread, buttered side uppermost. Sprinkle with remaining sugar.
4. Beat eggs and milk together and strain into dish over the bread. Leave to stand for 30 minutes. Place on low rack.
5. Cook for 18-20 minutes on DUAL COOK BAKE (on 200°C microwave MED-LOW), until the pudding is set and top is crisp and golden.

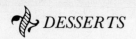

275g (10oz) plain flour
150g (5oz) fat, half margarine, half lard
2 x 15ml (2 tbsp) castor sugar
cold water to mix
450g (1 lb) fruit
sugar to taste

Fruit Pie

1. Sieve the flour, add sugar, cut the fat into cubes and rub into flour until the mixture resembles breadcrumbs. Add enough water to bind together and form a dough.
2. Line a pie plate 24cm (9½'') with half the pastry. Roll out remaining pastry for pie crust.
3. Prepare the fruit, place in a bowl, cover and cook for 6 minutes on HIGH.
4. Place filling in pastry case, place the lid onto filling and trim edges. Crimp and seal. Brush with egg or milk. Place on low rack.
5. Bake for 16-20 minutes on DUAL COOK BAKE (on 200°C microwave MED-LOW).

200ml (⅓pt) milk
2 eggs
50g (2oz) sugar
nutmeg - ground
100g (4oz) shortcrust pastry

Baked Custard Tart

1. Line a 21cm (8") pie dish with the pastry. Pierce the base and sides lightly.
2. Cook for 2-3 minutes on HIGH until partly cooked.
3. Whisk the eggs lightly with the sugar.
4. Warm the milk in the microwave for 1 minute on HIGH. Pour onto the egg mixture.
5. Strain the custard into the pastry case and sprinkle the surface with nutmeg. Place on low rack.
6. Cook for 11-13 minutes on DUAL COOK BAKE (on 200°C microwave MED-LOW).

225g (8oz) self raising flour
100g (4oz) suet
1 x 5ml (1 tsp) salt
150ml (¼pt) cold water
225g (8oz) jam

Jam Roly Poly

1. Sift the flour and salt into a mixing bowl.
2. Add the suet, mix to a dough with the cold water.
3. When mixed, lightly flour the work surface and roll the mixture into an oblong 1.25cm (½'') thick.
4. Spread jam over, leaving a small border around the edge. Roll up from the longest end. Place on a lightly greased dish. Cover with microwave plastic wrap.
5. Cook for 5-5½ minutes on HIGH.

37g (1½oz) plain flour
25g (1oz) castor sugar
25g (1oz) brown sugar
175g (6oz) mixed dried fruit
1 x 15ml (1 tbsp) black treacle
1 x size 3 egg
1 x 15ml (1 tbsp) brandy (or 5ml/1 tsp brandy essence)
1 x 15ml (1 tbsp) brown ale
37g (1½oz) shredded suet
37g (1½oz) breadcrumbs
25g (1oz) flaked almonds
juice and grated rind of 1 orange
1 x 5ml (1 tsp) mixed spice

Christmas Pudding

1. Line a 600ml (1pt) pudding dish with microwave plastic wrap.
2. Mix all ingredients together well, and spoon into the basin.
3. Cover the basin and cook for 8-9 minutes on MEDIUM.

Black Forest Gâteau

1. Soften margarine for 30 seconds - 1 minute on HIGH.
2. Cream with castor sugar.
3. Add beaten egg gradually, beat well after each addition.
4. Beat in grated carrot.
5. Fold in flour, baking powder and cocoa powder.
6. Stir in milk and gravy browning.
7. Spoon into 18cm (7'') plastic baking dish, base lined with kitchen roll.
8. Cook on upturned plate for 6-6½ minutes on HIGH.
9. Leave to stand for 5 minutes.
10. Slice into 2.

Soak base sponge with brandy. Fill with half the cream and black cherries. Decorate with remaining cream and black cherries.

125g (5oz) self raising flour
1 x 5ml (1 tsp) baking powder (sieved)
2 x 15ml (2 tbsp) cocoa powder
1 x 15ml (1 tbsp) milk
150g (5oz) margarine
150g (5oz) castor sugar
½ carrot - grated
1 x 5ml (1 tsp) gravy browning
3 x size 3 eggs - lightly beaten

Filling:
1 can black cherries
300ml (½pt) whipping cream
2 x 5ml (2 tsp) brandy

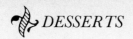

100g (4oz) margarine
100g (4oz) castor sugar
100g (4oz) self raising flour
1 x 5ml (1 tsp) baking powder
2 x size 2 eggs - beaten
3 x 15ml (3 tbsp) milk
3 x 15ml (3 tbsp) jam or syrup

Sponge Pudding with Sauce

1. Cream the margarine and castor sugar, then add the eggs slowly while still beating.
2. Add a tablespoon of sifted flour with the eggs and fold in the rest of the flour and baking powder.
3. Stir in the milk.
4. Grease and line the base of a 1 litre (2pt) dish and add cake mixture.
5. Cook for about 3-4 minutes on HIGH.
6. Place the jam or syrup in a glass bowl and heat for 30-45 seconds. Turn the sponge pudding out onto a serving dish and pour the sauce over. Serve.

450g (1 lb) fresh fruit
50g (2oz) brown sugar
1/2 x 5ml (1/2 tsp) cinnamon
175g (6oz) wholemeal flour
a pinch of salt
75g (3oz) butter or margarine
75g (3oz) brown sugar

Fruit Crumble

1. Place fruit, sugar and cinnamon in a dish.
2. Sieve flour and salt into a large mixing bowl, rub in fat until mixture resembles fine breadcrumbs. Add sugar and mix well. Sprinkle over fruit. Place on low metal rack.
3. Cook for 12-15 minutes on DUAL COOK ROAST (on 200°C microwave MEDIUM).

175g (6oz) plain flour
175g (6oz) castor sugar
1¼ x 5ml (1¼ tsp) baking powder
1/2 x 5ml (1/2 tsp) salt
1/4 x 5ml (1/4 tsp) bicarbonate of soda
75g (3oz) margarine or butter
180ml (6 fl oz) milk
1/2 x 5ml (1/2 tsp) vanilla essence
1 x size 3 egg
75g (3oz) chocolate melted

Topping:
50g (2oz) marshmallows
50g (2oz) plain chocolate
2 x 15ml (2 tbsp) golden syrup

Fudge Cake

1. Mix all the dry ingredients together. Add the remaining ingredients and mix together very well.
2. Line the base of a deep 18cm (7″) cake or soufflé dish. Pour the mixture in.
3. Stand on the low rack and cook for 6½-7½ minutes on HIGH. Leave to stand for 3 minutes before turning out.
4. Place marshmallows, chocolate and syrup in a bowl. Melt for 2 minutes on HIGH. Leave to thicken for 5 minutes.
5. Pour topping over cake.

50g (2oz) rice
25g (1oz) butter (optional)
600ml (1pt) milk
25g (1oz) castor sugar
nutmeg

Rice Pudding

1. Warm the milk for 2 minutes on HIGH.
2. Stir in the rice, sugar, and butter (if using).
3. Cook for 4 minutes on HIGH, or until boiling. Stir well.
4. Sprinkle the surface with nutmeg and reduce power to MED-LOW for 38-42 minutes.

Rich Cherry Cake

225g (8oz) plain flour
1/2 x 5ml (1/2 tsp) salt
1 x 5ml (1 tsp) baking powder
75g (3oz) glacé cherries
175g (6oz) butter or margarine
175g (6oz) castor sugar
2 x size 2 eggs
2 x 5ml (2 tsp) milk

1. Grease and line a deep 17.5cm (7'') cake tin.
2. Place butter or margarine, sugar, sieved flour, salt, baking powder in a bowl. Cut cherries into 4, add to dry ingredients. Add eggs.
3. Mix until light and fluffy. Add milk to form soft consistency. Place in cake tin and put it on the low rack.
4. Bake for 16-18 minutes on DUAL COOK (on 180°C microwave MED-LOW).
   Test if cake is cooked by using a skewer.

Chocolate Brownies

75g (3oz) butter
50g (2oz) cocoa
175 (6oz) soft brown sugar
2 x size 3 eggs - beaten
175g (6oz) plain flour
1/4 x 5ml (1/4 tsp) baking powder
1 x 5ml (1 tsp) vanilla essence
2 x 15ml (2 tbsp) cold milk
50g (2oz) walnuts - chopped

1. Melt butter in a glass bowl for 1½ minutes on HIGH. Stir.
2. Beat in sugar and eggs until the mixture is smooth.
3. Add flour sifted with baking powder and cocoa, vanilla essence and milk. Add walnuts.
4. Spread in greased glass dish 25 x 16 x 5cm (10 x 6½ x 2'').
5. Cook for 4-6 minutes on HIGH.
6. Allow to stand for 5 minutes and dust the top with sifted icing sugar.

Sachertorte

100g (4oz) butter
175g (6oz) dark cooking chocolate
175g (6oz) sugar
1 x 5ml (1 tsp) vanilla essence
6 x size 3 egg yolks
75g (3oz) flour
225g (8oz) eggs whites, stiffly whipped
6 x 15ml (6 tbsp) apricot jam
1 x 15ml (1 tbsp) water

Chocolate Icing:
225g (8oz) dark cooking chocolate
120ml (4 fl.oz.) double cream
350g (12oz) icing sugar

1. Grease and line a 23cm (9'') cake tin.
2. Mix the butter and sugar together until light and fluffy.
3. Melt the chocolate with 1 x 15ml (1 tbsp) of water for 1-2 minutes on HIGH.
4. Beat the melted chocolate into the mixture.
5. Add the vanilla essence and egg yolks gradually.
6. With a metal spoon fold in the flour, and then the egg whites.
7. Spoon the mixture into the prepared tin. Smooth over the top. Cook for 50-60 minutes on CONVECTION 180°C or until a skewer inserted into the centre of the cake comes out clean.
8. When the cake is cooked remove from the oven and allow to cool.
9. For the icing, melt the chocolate with 1 x 15ml (1 tbsp) of water for 1-2 minutes on HIGH.
10. Beat in the icing sugar and double cream. Mix thoroughly until the mixture is smooth.
11. Spread the apricot jam over the cake.
12. Cover the cake with the icing, ensuring the top and sides are covered. Smooth the icing with a flat-bladed knife.
13. Set aside to cool, until icing has set.

Coconut Clusters

100g (4oz) margarine
50g (2oz) castor sugar
1 x size 3 egg
150g (5oz) plain flour
150g (5oz) desiccated coconut
1 x 15ml (2 tbsp) jam-strawberry
(warm)
5 glacé cherries

1. In a large bowl beat together the margarine and sugar.
2. Add the egg and beat well. Mix in the plain flour and 25g (1oz) of coconut.
3. Place teaspoons of the mixture onto a lightly greased baking sheet.
4. Place on low rack and cook for 14-17 minutes on CONVECTION 200°C, until golden.
5. Allow to cool. Spread warmed jam over each biscuit.
6. Sprinkle coconut on top of each biscuit and decorate with a piece of glace cherry.

Shrewsbury Biscuits

100g (4oz) butter
100g (4oz) castor sugar
1 x size 3 egg - beaten
225g (8oz) plain flour
1 x 5ml (1 tsp) lemon juice

1. Cream the butter and sugar until fluffy. Add the eggs slowly beating after each addition.
2. Stir in the flour and lemon juice and mix to a firm dough. Roll out to 0.6cm (¼'') thick. Cut into rounds 6.3cm (2½'') place on a greased baking sheet and a turntable. Place the baking sheet on high rack.
3. Bake for 15-18 minutes on CONVECTION 200°C.

Variation on this basic dough:

Fruit Biscuits:
   100g (4oz) currants added to the mixture with the flour.

Spice Biscuits:
   Omit the lemon juice and add 1 x 5ml (1 tsp) mixed spice and 1 x 5ml (1 tsp) ground cinnamon to the flour.

Orange Biscuits:
   Replace the lemon juice with the juice of one orange.

Cherry Biscuits:
   Omit the lemon juice and add 50g (2oz) chopped glace cherries with the flour.

Quick Microwave Cake

100g (4oz) margarine
100g (4oz) castor sugar
100g (4oz) self raising flour
2 x size 3 eggs.
2-3 x 15ml (2-3 tbsp) water

1. In a large bowl cream together the sugar and margarine.
2. Add eggs, beat well.
3. Mix in the flour and add water.
4. Place in lined microwaveable container (approx 7" cake dish).
5. Cook for 4-5 minutes on HIGH.
6. Allow to stand for 5 minutes. Before removing from the container.
7. Decorate as required.

1 x 5ml (1 tsp) vegetable oil
75g (3oz) margarine
2 x 15ml (2 tbsp) golden syrup
75g (3oz) dark brown sugar
150g (5oz) porridge oats

Flap Jacks

1. Lightly grease with oil a 20cm (8'') shallow heat proof container.
2. In a heat proof dish place the margarine and syrup. Cook for 2-2½ minutes on HIGH until the margarine has melted.
3. Stir in dark brown sugar.
4. Stir in oats and mix well.
5. Pour the mixture into the prepared dish and level.
6. Cook for 2-2½ minutes on HIGH.
7. Remove from oven and mark into 8 portions. Allow to cool.
8. Cut into marked portions.

Florentines

50g (2oz) walnuts, chopped
50g (2oz) raisins
50g (2oz) glacé cherries, chopped
50g (2oz) almonds, chopped
25g (1oz) plain flour
50g (2oz) demerara sugar
50g (2oz) butter
1 x 15ml (1 tbsp) golden syrup

1. Melt butter, syrup and sugar together in a glass bowl for 1-2 minutes on HIGH.
2. Add all other ingredients together and mix well.
3. Place teaspoons of the mixture onto greased grease-proof paper on the turntable. Cook for 1½-2½ minutes on HIGH.
4. When cooked lift off the paper and allow to finish cooling. Repeat with remaining mixture.

Viennese Fingers

225g (8oz) butter
50g (2oz) icing sugar
325g (11oz) plain flour
2 egg yolks
4 drops of vanilla essence
100g (4oz) plain chocolate

1. Beat the butter until soft in a bowl. Add the sifted icing sugar and a little of the sifted flour and beat.
2. Gradually sift the remaining flour beating well each time.
3. Beat in the egg yolks and vanilla essence.
4. Place in a piping bag with a large star nozzle. Pipe onto a baking sheet and a turntable making each finger about 7.5cm (3'') long.
5. Place the baking sheet on high rack. Bake for 14-17 minutes on CONVECTION 200°C.
6. Leave to cool.
7. Place the chocolate in a bowl and cook for 1-1½ minutes on HIGH then beat well. Dip each end of the fingers in the chocolate and allow to cool on a wire rack.
8. Store in an airtight container.

Victoria Sandwich Cake

175g (6oz) butter or margarine
175g (6oz) castor sugar
3 x size 3 eggs
175g (6oz) self raising flour
40ml (2 tbsp) jam
castor sugar to dredge

1. Grease and line two 18cm (7'') sandwich tins.
2. Cream the fat and the sugar until pale and fluffy.
3. Add the eggs one at a time, beating well after each addition, fold in the flour with a metal spoon.
4. Halve the mixture and divide between the two prepared tins and smooth the tops. Place one tin on high rack.
5. Bake the cakes for 18-22 minutes on CONVECTION 180°C until golden brown and firm to the touch.
6. Turn out and cool on a wire rack.
7. When the cakes are cool sandwich them together with jam and sprinkle the top with castor sugar.

Variation to the basic cake mixture:

Chocolate:
Replace 3 x 15ml (3 tbsp) of flour with 3 x 15ml (3 tbsp) of cocoa. For a moist cake blend the cocoa with water to give a thick paste, and beat into the creamed ingredients.

Coffee:
Add 2 x 5ml (2 tsp) instant coffee dissolved in a little warm water to the creamed mixture.

Shortbread

100g (4oz) butter
50g (2oz) castor sugar or soft brown sugar
150g (5oz) plain flour
25g (1oz) semolina or ground rice

1. Cream butter and sugar, gradually work in the flour and semolina or ground rice with a fork. Knead well. Roll out until 1cm (½'') thick.
2. Cut into 6cm (2½'') rounds. Prick with fork. Place on greased baking sheet.
3. Heat for 2-3 minutes on HIGH. Cut into wedges and cool.

175ml (6 fl oz) corn oil
175g (6oz) castor sugar
3 x size 3 eggs
1 x 5ml (1 tsp) vanilla essence
225g (8oz) carrots
100g (4oz) walnut pieces - chopped
175g (6oz) plain flour
1 x 5ml (1 tsp) bicarbonate of soda
1 x 5ml (1 tsp) baking powder
1 x 5ml (1 tsp) cinnamon
1 x 5ml (1 tsp) salt

Passion Cake

1. Grease a 22cm (9'') cake tin.
2. Blend well the oil, sugar, eggs and vanilla essence in a bowl.
3. Add grated carrots, walnuts, flour, bicarbonate of soda, baking powder, salt and cinnamon.
4. Pour the batter into prepared tin and place on low rack. Bake for 23-28 minutes on DUAL COOK BAKE (on 200°C microwave MED-LOW).

100g (4oz) butter
100g (4oz) castor sugar
100g (4oz) plain flour
50g (2oz) ground almond
225g (8oz) mixed fruit
2 x size 3 eggs
1 x size 3 egg yolk

Lattice:
100g (4oz) marzipan
50g (2oz) glacé cherries halved
25g (1oz) walnut halves

Lattice Cake

1. Prepare a 19cm (7½'') loose bottom cake tin.
2. Cream butter and sugar together until fluffy. Gradually beat in the eggs, one at a time. Then beat in the extra egg yolk. Fold in the flour and ground almond and lastly the fruit. Turn the mixture into the prepared tin and level the surface.
3. Roll out the marzipan thinly, cut into strips and use to lattice the top of the cake. Fill each square with a halved cherry and walnut. Place on low rack.
4. Bake for 14-18 minutes on DUAL COOK BAKE (on 200°C microwave MED-LOW).

Sharp Christmas Cake

1. Line a 23cm (9'') cake tin using a double thickness of greaseproof paper.
2. Prepare fruit.
3. Cut the glacé pineapple and cherries into small cubes.
4. Cream the butter and sugar until fluffy and stir in the almonds.
5. Add the beaten eggs and black treacle.
6. Coat the fruits and peel in a little of the flour. Fold the fruit followed by the flour, walnuts, the grated orange rind and the orange juice, into the mixture.
7. Lastly, stir in the rum. Pour the mixture into the tin. Place on low rack.
8. Cook for 80-90 minutes on DUAL COOK (on 130°C microwave LOW).
9. Cool in the tin and store until required.

100g (4oz) walnuts
175g (6oz) glacé cherries - halved
225g (8oz) mixed dried fruit
100g (4oz) glacé pineapple
100g (4oz) candied mixed peel - chopped
225g (8oz) butter
225g (8oz) dark brown sugar
2 x 15ml (2 tbsp) treacle
50g (2oz) ground almonds
4 x size 3 eggs
225g (8oz) self raising flour
grated rind and juice of 1 orange
3 x 15ml (3 tbsp) rum

Simnel Cake

1. Line and grease a 17cm (7'') cake tin.
2. Take one third of the almond paste and roll it out to a round the size of the cake tin base.
3. Mix the prepared currants, sultanas, peel and cherries with the flour and baking powder, salt and spices. Cream the butter and sugar until pale and fluffy. Add the beaten eggs a little at a time beating well after each addition. Fold in half the flour and fruit using a tablespoon then fold in the rest of the flour mixture. Put half the mixture into the prepared tin.
4. Smooth and cover with the almond paste. Put the remaining cake mixture on top. Place on low rack.
5. Bake for 45-50 minutes on DUAL COOK (on 160°C microwave LOW).
6. After cooking decorate with the remainder of the almond paste.

50g (2oz) glacé cherries, quartered
450g (1 lb) almond paste
300g (10oz) currants
100g (4oz) sultanas
75g (3oz) mixed candied peel chopped
225g (8oz) plain flour
pinch of salt
1/2 x 5ml (1/2 tsp) baking powder
3 x 5ml (3 tsp) mixed spice
175g (6oz) butter
175g (6oz) soft brown sugar
3 x size 3 eggs beaten
milk to mix

50g (2oz) margarine
50g (2oz) castor sugar
1 x 15ml (1 tbsp) black treacle
100g (4oz) self raising flour
1 x 5ml (1 tsp) ground ginger
¼ x 5ml (¼ tsp) mixed spice
milk to mix

Ginger Biscuits

1. Cream the margarine and sugar together until light and fluffy. Beat in the treacle. Sieve the flour, ginger and spice onto the mixture. Fold in with a metal spoon and add a little milk if necessary. Turn onto a floured board and knead well. Roll out thinly and cut out with a cutter.
2. Place on a greased baking sheet and the turntable. Place the baking sheet on high rack. Cook for 15-17 minutes on CONVECTION 200°C. Leave on the sheet and the turntable for 3-4 minutes before putting onto cooling trays.
Makes approximately 25.

175g (6oz) butter
175g (6oz) castor sugar
3 x size 3 eggs - beaten
175g (6oz) self raising flour
1 orange - grated rind
1 x 15ml (1 tbsp) orange juice
50g (2oz) plain chocolate - broken into pieces
25g (1oz) cocoa

Marbled Chocolate Loaf

1. Grease and line a 2pt microwaveable loaf dish.
2. Cream butter and castor sugar together until light and fluffy. Beat in eggs beating well after each addition.
3. Fold in flour. Transfer half of mixture to a separate bowl and beat in orange rind and juice.
4. Place chocolate into a bowl and heat on HIGH for 2-3 minutes until melted. Stir well. Add this to remaining half of cake together with cocoa powder.
5. Put alternative spoonfuls of the two mixtures into prepared non-metallic loaf dish. Use a skewer to swirl through the mix to make a marbled effect. Level surface.
6. Cook on low metal rack for 6-7 minutes, on HIGH.
7. Allow to cool in dish for 3-5 minutes, cool on cooling rack.

225g (8oz) plain flour
pinch of salt
2 x 5ml (2 tsp) baking powder
grated rind of 1 lemon
150g (5oz) castor sugar
150g (5oz) butter
3 x size 2 eggs
3 x 15ml (3 tbsp) milk
a slice of lemon peel

Madeira Cake

1. Lightly grease a 18cm (7'') cake tin.
2. Sieve flour, salt and baking powder. Add lemon rind.
3. Cream sugar and butter until light and fluffy. Beat in eggs a little at a time.
4. Fold in dry ingredients. Add milk.
5. Place in prepared cake tin and place on low rack. Bake for 14-17 minutes on DUAL COOK BAKE (on 200°C microwave MED-LOW).

Parkin

1. Brush a 18cm (7'') square cake tin with melted fat, line base and sides with greaseproof paper, brush with more fat.
2. Sift flour, salt, spice, cinnamon, ground ginger, and bicarbonate of soda into a bowl. Add oatmeal. Make a well in the centre.
3. Put treacle, butter, sugar and milk in a heatproof bowl and cook for 3 minutes on HIGH.
4. Pour into the well and add the egg. Stir mixture briskly without beating until smooth and evenly combined.
5. Transfer to tin and place on low rack. Bake for 13-16 minutes on DUAL COOK BAKE (on 200°C microwave MED-LOW).
6. Cool on a wire rack, store without removing paper in an air-tight tin for about one week before cutting.

175g (6oz) plain flour
1/2 x 5ml (1/2 tsp) salt
1 x 5ml (1 tsp) each, mixed spice,
cinnamon and ground ginger
1 x 5ml (1 tsp) bicarbonate of soda
275g (10oz) medium oatmeal
175g (6oz) black treacle
150g (5oz) butter
100g (4oz) soft brown sugar
150ml (1/4pt) milk
1 x size 3 egg, beaten

Boiled Fruit Cake

1. Place into a bowl, the margarine, dark brown sugar, mixed fruit, water, bicarbonate of soda, gravy browning and mixed spice. Mix together and cook for 3 minutes on HIGH. Allow to cool.
2. To the beaten egg, add the water. Mix the egg, water and self-raising flour to the other ingredients.
3. Stir the mixture thoroughly. Line the base of a 8cm (7") soufflé dish with greaseproof paper. Pour the ingredients into the soufflé dish.
4. Cook for 19-23 minutes on MED-LOW.
5. Leave the cake to stand for 5 minutes.

75g (3oz) margarine
100g (4oz) dark brown sugar
250g (9oz) mixed fruit
180ml (6 fl oz) water
1/2 x 5ml (1/2 tsp) bicarbonate of soda
1 x 5ml (1 tsp) mixed spice
1/2 x 5ml (1/2 tsp) gravy browning
1 x size 3 egg - beaten
1 x 15ml (1 tbsp) water
175g (6oz) self raising flour

Swiss Roll

1. Grease and line a 23 x 15cm (9 x 6'') oblong dish.
2. Whisk eggs and sugar together until the mixture is pale and a trail can be seen in the mixture when the whisk is lifted out.
3. Quickly fold in the flour. Pour the mixture into the prepared dish.
4. Cook for 2 minutes on HIGH placed on the low metal rack.
5. Cut a piece of greaseproof paper out just larger than the dish. Sprinkle it with the 1 x 15ml (1 tbsp) of castor sugar.
6. Turn the swiss roll out onto the sugared greaseproof and carefully remove the lining paper.
7. Spread the jam evenly over the surface of the swiss roll.
8. Roll it up lengthways, as tightly as possible. Place on a serving dish.

50g (2oz) castor sugar
2 x size 3 eggs
50g (2oz) plain flour
2 x 15ml (2 tbsp) strawberry or
raspberry jam
1 x 15ml (1 tbsp) castor sugar

100g (4oz) self raising flour
100g (4oz) margarine
100g (4oz) castor sugar
2 x size 3 eggs
pink food colouring
2 x 15ml (2 tbsp) raspberry/strawberry jam
225g (8oz) marzipan

Battenburg

1. Mix flour, margarine, sugar and eggs together well with a fork.
2. Divide the mixture in half. Colour one half of the mixture with pink colouring.
3. Place one half of the mixture into a small rectangular shaped dish approx 15 x 5cm (6 x 2''). Cook for 2 minutes on HIGH placed on a rack or upturned saucer.
4. When cooked remove from dish and repeat with other half of mixture.
5. When cakes are cooled cut each in half lengthways. Place a pink piece of cake next to a yellow piece. Brush a little jam on the top and sides of cake touching each other. Then place a yellow piece of cake on top of the pink piece and vice versa.
6. Roll out the marzipan.
7. Brush all the exposed sides of the cake with jam (if the jam is stiff melt for 30 seconds on HIGH).
8. Cover the sides and edges with marzipan.

Milk Bread

1 x 5ml (1 tsp) sugar
15g (1/2oz) fresh yeast
300ml (1/2pt) hand hot milk
450g (1 lb) strong plain flour
1 x 5ml (1 tsp) salt
40g (11/2oz) butter

1. Dissolve the sugar and yeast in half the milk. Sift the flour and salt into a bowl, rub in the butter, then make a well in the centre. Pour in the yeast liquid and the remaining milk and mix into a pliable dough.
2. Turn the dough out onto a floured surface and knead for 10 minutes until smooth.
3. Put the dough into a lightly greased polythene bag and leave in a warm place until doubled in bulk, or put into a bowl and prove on the proof cycle. (40°C, 30 minutes).
4. Shape the dough into an oblong and place into the greased (900g (2 lb)) loaf tin. Place on low rack.
5. Bake for 10-16 minutes on DUAL COOK BAKE (on 200°C microwave MED-LOW).

Wholemeal Loaf

675g (11/2 lb) wholemeal flour
15g (1/2oz) lard
1 x 15ml (1 tbsp) castor sugar
15g (1/2oz) dried yeast
450ml (3/4pt) water, hand hot
2 x 5ml (2 tsp) salt

1. Place flour in a non-metal bowl, heat for 1 minute on HIGH. Rub lard into flour.
2. Sprinkle with 1 x 5ml (1 tsp) sugar and yeast into 150ml (1/4pt) of the water.
   Leave in a warm place for 10-15 minutes until the mixture is frothy. Pour remaining sugar and salt into remaining water. Add to flour with yeast mixture. Knead for 5 minutes until dough is smooth and elastic. Cover dough with polythene bag, leave in a warm place for 30 minutes or until doubled in size or use proof cycle (40°C, 30 minutes). Knead for a further 5 minutes, divide into two. Shape and place in two greased 1kg (2 lb) loaf tins. Leave in a warm place until dough has doubled in size. Place two tins on low rack. Bake for 12-16 minutes on DUAL COOK BAKE (on 200°C microwave MED-LOW).

Quick Wholemeal Rolls

300ml (1/2pt) water (approx)
1 x 5ml (1 tsp) sugar
450g (1 lb) wholemeal flour
2 x 5ml (2 tsp) salt
25g (1oz) lard
15g (1/2oz) fresh yeast

1. Activate the yeast in 150ml (1/4pt) of the water with the sugar. Mix the flour and salt and rub in the fat.
2. Add the yeast mixture and remaining water and mix to a fairly soft dough, adding more water if necessary.
3. Beat and knead well and divide into 10-12 portions. Shape into rolls on a greased baking sheet. Prove on proof cycle (40°C, 30 minutes). Place on low rack.
4. Bake for 11-16 minutes on DUAL COOK BAKE (on 200°C microwave MED-LOW) until brown.

Soda Bread

100g (4oz) wholemeal flour
175g (6oz) plain flour
½ x 5ml (½ tsp) salt
1 x 5ml (1 tsp) bicarbonate of soda
2 x 5ml (2 tsp) cream of tartar
25g (1oz) margarine
150ml (¼pt) milk

1. Sift all dry ingredients into a bowl. Rub in margarine finely.
2. Mix with milk to form a soft but not sticky dough. Knead lightly. Place on a large dinner plate, pat out into a circle approx 20cm (8'').
3. Divide into 8 wedges and almost cut through with a knife. Place on low rack. Cook for 16-19 minutes on DUAL COOK (on 200°C microwave LOW). Eat on day of making. Makes 8 portions.

Fruit Scones

225g (8oz) self raising flour
50g (2oz) sugar
50g (2oz) butter
50g (2oz) sultanas
150ml (¼pt) milk - made up with 1 x size 3 egg (beaten)

1. In a bowl sieve the flour, add the sugar, mix well.
2. Rub in the butter.
3. Add the sultanas. Mix to a smooth dough with the egg and milk mixture.
4. Roll out the dough and cut into rounds 1cm (½'') deep.
5. Place on a greased baking sheet and cook for 15-18 minutes DUAL COOK (on 200°C microwave LOW).

Cheese and Chive Scones

225g (8oz) self raising flour
pinch of salt
50g (2oz) butter
100g (4oz) mature cheddar - grated
15ml (1 tbsp) chives
150ml (¼pt) fresh milk
1 x 15ml (1 tbsp) milk

1. In a bowl sift the flour and salt, add butter, rub in until it resembles fine breadcrumbs.
2. Mix in 75g (3oz) of the cheese and chives.
3. Add 150ml (¼pt) of the milk and mix to a soft dough, knead slightly until smooth.
4. Roll on a floured work surface until a 0.5'' (1cm) thick round shape is formed.
5. Score into 8 pieces using a sharp knife.
6. Place on baking sheet.
7. Brush with milk, sprinkle over remaining cheese.
8. Bake on DUAL COOK (on 200°C microwave MED-LOW) for 15 minutes.

Caribbean Tea Loaf

225g (8oz) self raising flour
½ x 5ml (½ tsp) salt
½ x 5ml (½ tsp) mixed spice
100g (4oz) butter - cut into pieces
50g (2oz) mixed fruit
50g (2oz) coconut - desiccated
450g (1 lb) bananas - peeled
1 x 15ml (1 tbsp) runny honey
2 x size 3 eggs - beaten

1. In a bowl sieve the flour salt and mixed spice. Rub in the butter so that it resembles fine breadcrumbs.
2. Stir in the mixed fruit and coconut. In a small bowl mash the bananas, add the honey and stir well. Add to the dry ingredients.
3. Mix well together with the beaten eggs.
4. Pour the mixture into a lightly greased 1kg (2 lb) loaf tin.
5. Cook for 30-35 minutes DUAL COOK (on 160°C microwave LOW) until cooked.
6. Cool slightly in tin, remove from tin and allow to cool on wire rack.

225g (8oz) wholemeal flour
pinch of salt
½ x 5ml (½ tsp) cream of tartar
50g (2oz) margarine or butter
25g (1oz) sugar
75g (3oz) currants
150ml (¼pt) milk
1 x size 3 egg - beaten

Wholemeal Scones

1. Sieve the flour, salt and cream of tartar into a bowl, mix together. Rub the fat into the flour add the sugar and dried fruit.
2. Gradually add the milk until a soft consistency is reached. Form the mixture into a ball.
3. Roll out the mixture into a 20cm (8″) circle, ½-1cm (¼-½″) thick. Mark into even portions. Brush with the beaten egg.
4. Place on a greased baking sheet. Place on low rack. Cook for 10-14 minutes on DUAL COOK (on 200°C microwave LOW). Glaze the wholemeal scone with honey - if required.

100g (4oz) bran
100g (4oz) soft brown sugar (dark)
225g (8oz) mixed fruit
300ml (½pt) milk
175g (6oz) self raising flour
2 x 15ml (2 tsp) mixed spice

Bran Teabread

1. Line a 1200ml (2pt) loaf dish.
2. Combine all the ingredients together.
3. Pour the mixture into the prepared loaf dish.
4. Cook for 7-8 minutes on HIGH. Leave to cool.
5. Turn out of the loaf dish.

Hot Cross Buns

1. Froth the dried yeast in the warm liquid with 1 x 5ml (1 tsp) of the sugar, or crumble the fresh yeast into the warm liquid with 1 x 5ml (1 tsp) of the sugar.
2. Sift the remaining sugar, flour, salt and spices together and rub in the margarine. Make a well in the centre of the flour mixture and pour in the yeast liquid and mix to form a dough.
3. Knead the dough until smooth and elastic. Place in a bowl, cover and prove until double in size on the proof cycle (40°C, 30 minutes).
4. Add the fruit and re-knead. Divide the dough into 12 pieces and shape into buns. Place well apart on a greased baking sheet. Prove again for 15 minutes on the proof cycle (40°C, 15 minutes).
5. To make paste mix all ingredients together well and place in a piping bag with a small plain nozzle. Cut crosses on the buns and then pipe the paste.
6. Place on low rack. Bake for 13-17 minutes on DUAL COOK BAKE (on 200°C microwave MED-LOW). When the buns have cooked place on cooling rack.
7. Make the glaze by heating the castor sugar and milk together and heat for 1 minute until hot. Brush the buns with the hot glaze. Leave to cool.

25g (1oz) fresh yeast or 1 x 15ml (1 tbsp) dried yeast
75g (3oz) castor sugar
450g (1 lb) strong plain flour
½ x 5ml (½ tsp) salt
½ x 5ml (½ tsp) ground nutmeg
1 x 5ml (1 tsp) ground cinnamon
1 x 5ml (1 tsp) mixed spice
75g (3oz) margarine
1 egg beaten made up to 250ml (½pt) with milk and warm water
100g (4oz) currants
50g (2oz) chopped mixed peel

Paste:
25g (1oz) margarine
50g (2oz) plain flour
4 x 15ml (4 tbsp) water

Glaze:
40g (1½oz) castor sugar
75ml (3 fl oz) milk and water

Swedish Tea Ring

1. Mix yeast with 5ml (1 tsp) of castor sugar and the warm water. Leave for about 5 minutes to froth.
2. Place milk, butter and remaining castor sugar in a heatproof dish. Heat for 1-2 minutes on HIGH until butter is melted. Allow to cool until luke warm.
3. In a large bowl place sifted flour, salt, yeast mixture and cooled milk. Mix well, then add eggs. Knead until smooth about 5-10 minutes.
4. Leave to prove for 45-60 minutes until doubled in size. Knock back and knead again until smooth. Roll out to a rectangle 30 x 20cm (12 x 8″) and 1.5cm (½″) thick.
5. Melt butter for 30-45 seconds on HIGH. Brush the dough with the butter. Scatter over sultanas, almonds and mixed spice. Roll dough to form a 30cm (12″) length. Brush ends with water to form a circle.
6. Place ring with folded edge downwards onto a lightly greased baking sheet. Using a sharp knife make deep cuts downwards approximately ⅔ way through ring at 5cm (2″) intervals. Twist each portion slightly to reveal fillings.
7. Cook on low metal rack for 18-22 minutes on DUAL COOK (on 200°C microwave MED-LOW).
8. Allow to cool. Mix icing sugar with cold water to form a stiff paste. Decorate top of ring with icing, almonds, cherries etc. Serve.

25g (1oz) fresh yeast or 12g (½oz) dried yeast
25g (1oz) castor sugar
60ml (4 tbsp) luke warm water
250ml (8 fl oz) milk
100g (4oz) butter
675g (1¼ lb) strong white flour - sifted
2 x 5ml (2 tsp) salt
2 x size 3 eggs - lightly beaten
25g (1oz) butter
175g (6oz) sultanas or raisins
50g (2oz) flaked almonds
2 x 5ml (2 tsp) mixed spice
100g (4oz) icing sugar
flaked almonds, glacé cherries, angelica to decorate

2 sheets of puff pastry (20cm/8"
square)
sweet mincemeat
raspberry jam
cooking apple
50g (2oz) icing sugar
glacé cherries, flaked almonds, angelica
30ml (2 tbsp) milk

Quick Danish Pastries

1. Cut each square into 4 smaller squares. With four of the small squares, make 2.5cm (1") cut diagonally into each corner. In the centre place either a spoonful of jam or mincemeat or same small slices of cooking apple. Fold alternate corners into the centre. Brush with the milk to secure.
2. With remaining 4 small squares, place the filling (as above) on one corner of the square, folding the other side over to make a triangular pastry shape. Secure edges with milk.
3. Place all 8 pastries onto a baking sheet and cook on the low rack for 10-12 minutes DUAL COOK (on 200°C microwave LOW).
4. Allow to cool.
5. Mix icing sugar with 2 x 15ml (2 tbsp) cold water. Decorate top of pastries with icing, cherries, angelica or almonds.

350g (12oz) self raising flour
40g (1½oz) soft brown sugar
75g (3oz) seedless raisins
40g (1½oz) walnuts, finely chopped
40g (1½oz) black treacle
75g (3oz) malt extract
225ml (8 fl oz) fresh milk

Malt Loaf

1. Sift the flour into a mixing bowl, add the sugar, raisins and walnuts.
2. Blend together the treacle, malt extract and milk. Cook for 2-3 minutes on HIGH. Stir gradually into the flour and beat until smooth.
3. Spoon the mixture into a greased and floured 1kg (2 lb) loaf tin and smooth over the top. Place on low rack.
4. Cook for 18-23 minutes on DUAL COOK BAKE (on 200°C microwave MED-LOW).

675g (1½ lb) strong white flour
2 x 5ml (2 tsp) salt
1 x 15ml (1 tbsp) lard
2 x 5ml (2 tsp) dried yeast
1 x 5ml (1 tsp) castor sugar
450ml (¾pt) milk and water

Crisp Bread Rolls

1. Sift flour and salt together into a large mixing bowl. Cut lard into small pieces and rub into flour.
2. Stir sugar into milk and water. Heat for 1½-2 minutes on HIGH until the mixture is hand hot. Sprinkle yeast into liquid. Leave for 10 minutes or until the mixture is frothy.
3. Make a well in the centre of the flour, pour in the yeast liquid. Combine all ingredients into a ball. Knead well for 10 minutes. Place in a greased bowl, place in proof cycle (40°C, 30 minutes).
4. Knead dough for a further 5 minutes. Divide mixture into 12 pieces. Shape into rolls and place on baking sheet. Leave in a warm place until the rolls have doubled in size. Brush with salted water. Place on low rack.
5. Bake for 16-20 minutes on DUAL COOK BAKE (on 200°C microwave MED-LOW). Repeat with remaining rolls.

PRESERVES AND
SWEETS

Rhubarb Jam

450g (1 lb) rhubarb - trimmed weight
450g (1 lb) granulated sugar
juice from 1 lemon

1. Chop the rhubarb into short even-sized lengths.
2. Arrange in a large bowl. Alternate the rhubarb and sugar in layers.
3. Pour the lemon juice over and cover with microwave plastic wrap. Leave overnight in a cool place.
4. Remove the cover and place the bowl with the rhubarb in the microwave and cook for 18-22 minutes on HIGH, until setting point is reached. Stir after 3 minutes, so that the sugar is dissolved.
5. Pour into pots. Cover, seal and label.

Strawberry Jam

450g (1 lb) strawberries
1 x 15ml (1 tbsp) lemon juice
350g (12oz) sugar

1. Wash and hull strawberries. Put into a 2.8 litre (5pt) mixing bowl with the lemon juice.
2. Cook for 4½-5 minutes on HIGH, or until fruit is soft. Add sugar and stir well.
3. Cook for 12-14 minutes on HIGH, or until setting point is reached.
4. Cool slightly before putting in clean warm jar. Makes approx ½kg (1 lb). Cover. Seal and label.

Plum Jam

900g (2 lb) plums, halved and stoned
300ml (½pt) water
1 x 15ml (1 tbsp) lemon juice
900g (2 lb) castor sugar

1. Place plums and water in a large bowl. Cook for 8-9 minutes on HIGH or until fruit is soft.
2. Add lemon juice and sugar, stir until sugar dissolved. Bring to boil and then cook for 18-23 minutes on HIGH until setting point is reached.
3. Allow to cool slightly before putting in warm jars, and cover. Makes approx. 1½kg (3 lb)

Raspberry Jam Plus

600g (1 lb 4oz) frozen raspberries
600g (1 lb 4oz) castor sugar
1 x 15ml (1 tbsp) lemon juice

1. Place frozen raspberries in a 2-litre (4pt) casserole. Cook on HIGH until thawed, 2-4 minutes. Stir in sugar and lemon juice. Cook on HIGH until mixture boils, 9-11 minutes stirring after half the cooking time.
2. Microwave on HIGH until mixture comes to a rolling boil, 3-4 minutes. Microwave on HIGH to continue boiling, 1 minute. Pour into prepared jars, seal and refrigerate.

Seville Orange Marmalade

675g (1½ lb) seville oranges
1 lemon - juice & pips
900ml (1½pt) water
1½kg (3 lb) sugar

1. Wash fruit well. Using a potato peeler or sharp knife, remove rind from oranges and cut into thin strips. Halve oranges and lemon, squeeze juice and remove pips. Cut fruit into pieces. Tie fruit pieces into a piece of clean muslin with pips from oranges and lemon.
2. Place rind, juice and water into a large bowl add muslin bag. Cover bowl with microwave plastic wrap. Cook for 16-18 minutes on HIGH, until rind is soft. Remove muslin bag.
3. Stir in sugar. Heat on HIGH, until sugar has dissolved, stirring regularly. Bring to the boil.
4. Cook for 20-25 minutes on HIGH or until a set is obtained. Allow to cool slightly before potting. Cover.
Makes approx. 2¼ kg (5 lb).

Date Chutney

250g (½ lb) dates - stoned and roughly chopped
250g (½ lb) currants
1 medium onion - peeled and chopped
150g (6oz) brown sugar
2 cloves of garlic - crushed
2 x 5ml (2 tsp) salt
1 x 5ml (1 tsp) chilli powder
300ml (½pt) vinegar

1. Place all the above ingredients in a large bowl.
2. Cook for 15-19 minutes on HIGH, until the dates and currants are tender.
3. Mix with a spoon until the desired consistency is reached.
4. Leave to cool.
5. Pot, seal and label the chutney.

Piccalilli

225g (8oz) cucumber - cubed
225g (8oz) under-ripe tomatoes - chopped
225g (8oz) onions or shallots - chopped
225g (8oz) cauliflower florets
225g (8oz) courgettes
1200ml (2pt) water
25g (1oz) salt
25g (1oz) plain flour
75g (3oz) sugar
2 x 5ml (1 tsp) mustard
2 x 5ml (1 tsp) turmeric

1. Place all vegetables in a large bowl and add the salt and water. Cover and leave overnight.
2. Add spices to the vinegar in a basin and cook for 8-10 minutes on HIGH, stir once half way through.
3. Drain and rinse the vegetables and place in a large covered bowl, cook for 5-6 minutes on HIGH.
4. Blend flour, mustard, sugar and turmeric with a little of the spiced vinegar to make a smooth paste.
5. Heat remaining spiced vinegar for 2 minutes on HIGH. Pour onto blended mixture and cook for a further 2 minutes.
6. Pour vinegar mixture over vegetables and cook on HIGH for 21 minutes, stir half way through.
7. Allow to stand before bottling. Cover seal and label.

For spiced vinegar:

600ml (1pt) malt vinegar
3 peppercorns
3 whole cloves
¼ x 5ml (¼ tsp) allspice
½ x 5ml (½ tsp) cinnamon
½ x 5ml (½ tsp) chilli powder

Apricot Chutney

225g (8oz) dried apricots
175g (6oz) sultanas
75g (3oz) onion - chopped
1 x 5ml (1 tsp) salt
½ x 5ml (½ tsp) mixed spice
1 x 5ml (1 tsp) ground ginger
¼ x 5ml (¼ tsp) cayenne pepper
100g (4oz) brown sugar
300ml (½pt) brown malt vinegar

1. Place dried apricots in a large bowl, cover with water and cook uncovered for 6-7 minutes on HIGH. Stand for 5 minutes. Drain, but reserve syrup.
2. Chop apricots, add sultanas, onion, salt, spices and pepper and 2 x 15ml (2 tbsp) of the apricot syrup. Cook, uncovered for 8-9 minutes on HIGH.
3. Add sugar and vinegar and cook, uncovered for 14-16 minutes on HIGH or until thickened. Stir twice during cooking.
4. Fill warm jars with chutney and cover. Makes approx. 1kg (2 lb).

Green Tomato Chutney

675g (1½ lb) green tomatoes
175g (6oz) onion, chopped
2 x 5ml (2 tsp) salt
1-2 x 5ml (1-2 tsp) ground ginger
½ x 5ml (½ tsp) cayenne pepper
350g (12oz) sultanas or seedless raisins
225g (8oz) brown sugar
600ml (1pt) brown malt vinegar

1. Chop or mince tomatoes and onions. Place in a large bowl with salt, spices, pepper and sultanas. Cover and cook for 12-14 minutes on HIGH or until pulped.
2. Add sugar and vinegar and cook for 40-45 minutes on HIGH or until consistency is like jam.
3. Fill warmed jars with chutney and cover. Makes approx. 1½kg (3 lb).

Variation: Use quartered apples or a ½ and ½ mixture of apples and tomatoes in place of tomatoes

Fudge

350g (12oz) semi-sweet or milk chocolate chips
200g (1 can) condensed sweetened milk
25g (1oz) margarine or butter
100g (4oz) roughly chopped walnuts

1. Place all ingredients except nuts in a large bowl.
2. Cook for 4-6 minutes on MEDIUM or until chocolate has melted, stirring once or twice during cooking. Stir in nuts. Pour into a well-greased baking dish, 20 x 20cm (8 x 8″). Refrigerate until set.

Blackberry Jelly

450g (1 lb) blackberries
450ml (¾pt) water
1 lemon - juice of
sugar - as required

N.B. For every 600ml (1pt) of juice extract you will require
450g (1 lb) sugar

1. Mix the blackberries, water and lemon juice together in a heat-proof bowl.
2. Cook for 17-19 minutes on HIGH.
3. Strain the mixture. Throw the pulp away. Reserve the remaining liquid.
4. Add the sugar - amount as required. Stir until dissolved.
5. Cook the mixture for 18-24 minutes on HIGH or until setting point is reached. Stirring every 5 minutes.
6. Pot, seal and label the jelly.

75g (3oz) golden syrup
100g (4oz) castor sugar
4 x 15ml (4 tbsp) water
1½ x 5ml (1½ tsp) baking powder
25g (1oz) margarine or butter
225g (8oz) shelled raw peanuts

Peanut Brittle

1. Grease a baking sheet heavily. Combine sugar, syrup and water in a glass bowl. Microwave for 3 minutes on HIGH stirring frequently.
2. Add baking powder and margarine or butter and microwave on HIGH for 1 minute.
3. Stir in peanuts and microwave for 5-6 minutes on HIGH. Stirring after each 1-1½ minutes until it reaches 'crack' stage.
4. Spread onto baking sheet. Cool and refrigerate. Break into pieces.

225g (8oz) demerara sugar
1 x 15ml (1 tbsp) treacle
25g (1oz) butter
2 x 15ml (2 tbsp) vinegar
5 x 15ml (5 tbsp) water

Treacle Toffee

1. Dissolve the sugar, water, treacle, butter and vinegar together in a dish. Cook for 6-9 minutes on HIGH until the toffee reaches the crack stage.
2. Pour into a greased tin and mark into squares. Allow to set 2-3 hours.

225g (8oz) demerara sugar
1 x 15ml (1 tbsp) syrup
25g (1oz) butter
2 x 15ml (2 tbsp) malt vinegar
5 x 15ml (5 tbsp) water
4 eating apples

Toffee Apples

1. Place sugar, water, syrup, butter and vinegar in a bowl and cook for 6-9 minutes on HIGH. Stir regularly until toffee reaches hard crack. Test toffee by dropping a little in cold water.
2. Dip the apples in the toffee mixture and leave on greaseproof paper to set.

100g (4oz) butter
3 x eggs, size 3
225g (8oz) castor sugar
finely grated rind and juice of 3 lemons

Lemon Curd

1. Heat butter for 3 minutes on HIGH until melted.
2. Beat remaining ingredients together and add to melted butter, stir well. Cook for 5-6 minutes on HIGH, stirring half way through cooking time. When cooked sufficiently the curd should be thick enough to coat the back of a spoon.
3. Allow to cool slightly before transforming into warmed jars. Cover when cold. Makes approx. ½kg (1 lb).

175g (6oz) lean pork - cubed
4 button mushrooms
¼ red pepper - cut into 4
¼ green pepper - cut into 4
1 small onion - quartered

For the marinade
1 x 15ml (1 tbsp) runny honey
1 x 15ml (1 tbsp) soy sauce
½ x 5ml (½ tsp) ground ginger

Pork Kebabs

1. Skewer the pork, mushrooms, red and green peppers and onion onto the wood skewers.
2. Mix all other ingredients together.
3. Place kebabs onto a large plate, poor over marinade, and leave to stand for at least 2-3 hours.
4. Brush kebabs with marinade and then place kebabs onto high wire rack.
5. Cook on DUAL COOK GRILL (microwave MEDIUM/GRILL) for 10-11 minutes, turning ½ way through cooking time. Serve on a bed of rice.

2 spring cabbage leaves - thinly sliced
1 small onion - peeled and chopped
1 carrot - peeled and chopped
50g (2oz) long grain rice
1 celery stick - chopped
25g (1oz) butter
25g (1oz) mange tout - chopped
1 slice ham - cut into strips
1 x 5ml (tsp) soy sauce
1pt hot water

Vegetable Risotto

1. Heat butter in a non-metallic dish for 30 seconds on HIGH.
2. Add the onions, carrot, mange tout, cabbage leaves, and celery. Mix in butter and cook on HIGH for 2 minutes.
3. Add rice and heat for 1 minute on HIGH.
4. Add ham, soy sauce and pour water over.
Season to taste and cook for 15 minutes on HIGH stirring half way through.

1 salmon steak (approximately 225g)
1 x 15ml (1 tbsp) natural yoghurt
1 x 5ml (1 tsp) honey
1 x 5ml (1 tsp) whole grain mustard
1 x 5ml (1 tsp) lemon juice
1 clove garlic - chopped
1 x 5ml (1 tsp) dill
1x 5ml (1 tsp) pecan nuts - chopped
salt and pepper

12" square greaseproof paper

Salmon Steak en Papillote

1. Combine yoghurt, honey, mustard, lemon juice, garlic and dill.
2. Place salmon steak in centre of greaseproof paper. Pour over yoghurt sauce. Season and sprinkle over pecan nuts.
3. Gather together cones of paper and fold over to make a seal.
4. Place on microwaveable plate and cook on HIGH for 2½-3 minutes.
5. Allow to stand for 2-3 minutes before undoing paper.

2 slices lightly toasted bread
12g (½oz) butter - optional
40g (1½oz) cooked pasta (eg. spaghetti/maccaroni)
175g (6oz) cheddar cheese (cubed)
¼ x 5ml (¼ tsp) ground mace
pinch powdered mustard
2½ x 15ml (2½ tbsp) beer or milk
seasoning

Pasta Rarebit

1. In a non-metallic bowl place the cheese, ground mace, mustard and butter (optional).
2. Heat for 1-2 minutes on HIGH until melted. Add beer or milk.
3. Mix well. Add cooked pasta. Mix until thick and creamy. Season to taste.
4. Place pasta mixture onto the toast. Place toast on high metal rack. Place under the grill for 4-6 minutes until golden.

Stir Fry Chicken

1. Cut chicken into thin strips.
2. Place oil in a large casserole. Add onion and carrot and chicken. Cook for 3-4 minutes on HIGH.
3. Add broccoli, sweetcorn and beansprouts. Cook for 3-4 minutes on HIGH. Add soya sauce and stir. Season.
4. Heat through for 1 minute on HIGH. Serve.

175g (6oz) chicken breast fillet
50g (2oz) onion finely chopped
50g (2oz) beansprouts
50g (2oz) sweetcorn kernals
50g (2oz) broccoli
50g (2oz) carrot cut into julienne strips
1 x 15ml (1 tbsp) oil
1 x 15ml (1 tbsp) soya sauce
seasoning

Stuffed Jacket Potatoes

1. Pierce jacket potatoes. Wrap in kitchen paper and place on turntable. Cook for 7-11 minutes on HIGH. Allow to stand for 5 minutes.
2. Cut potatoes in half and remove the cooked potato and place in a bowl. Add the butter seasoning and cream and mash potatoes until smooth.
3. Add grated cheese, ham and chopped pepper and mix well.
4. Spoon into potato shells. Place on a plate and cook for 2-3 minutes on HIGH. Serve.

2 medium potatoes
50g (2oz) grated cheddar cheese
25g (1oz) butter
50g (2oz) ham chopped
50g (2oz) chopped green pepper
seasoning
2 x 15ml (2 tbsp) single cream

Gammon Steak with Mustard Sauce

1. Place gammon steak on a plastic rack. Cook for 2-3 minutes on HIGH. Stand and cover the gammon.
2. Place butter in a large jug and melt for 30 seconds on HIGH. Mix in the flour and mustard. Stir in the milk. Cook for 1½-2½ minutes on HIGH.
3. Whisk sauce until smooth. Pour over gammon and serve.

150g (5oz) gammon steak
150ml (¼pt) milk
12g (½ oz) butter
12g (½ oz) plain flour
1 x 5ml (1 tsp) dry mustard
salt and pepper

Plaice with Mushrooms

1. Roll plaice fillet up. Skin side inwards tail to head. Place in a small casserole.
2. Mix mushrooms with condensed soup. Season and pour over fish.
3. Cover and cook for 4-6 minutes on MED-HIGH.

150g (6oz) plaice fillet
50g (2oz) mushrooms - sliced
1 small can condensed mushroom soup
salt and pepper

1 medium sized baking apple
1 x 15ml (1 tbsp) sweet mincemeat
1 x 15ml (1 tbsp) flaked almonds

Baked Apple

1. Core the apple with an apple corer. Cut round the skin of the apple to prevent splitting.
2. Place mincemeat and almonds in the centre of the apple. Place on a plate.
3. Cover and cook for 2-3½ minutes on HIGH.

1 large banana
1 x 15ml (1 tbsp) butter
1 x 15ml (1 tbsp) brown sugar
1 x 15ml (1 tbsp) orange juice
1 x 15ml (1 tbsp) rum

Bananas in Rum

1. Place brown sugar and butter in a glass bowl and heat for 1-2 minutes on HIGH.
2. Add the orange juice and rum. Stir and mix together.
3. Slice banana in half and place in serving dish. Pour over sauce.
4. Heat for 1-2 minutes on HIGH. Serve with cream.

4 slices bread
25g (1oz) butter
25g (1oz) sultanas
25g (1oz) castor sugar
2 x 15ml (2 tbsp) preserve (eg. lemon curd/strawberry jam)
1 x size 3 egg
¼pt milk

Sweet Butter Pudding

1. Remove crusts from the bread and spread slices thickly with butter. Cut into squares.
2. Place half of the bread, buttered side uppermost into a lightly greased small casserole dish.
3. Sprinkle with fruit and half the sugar.
4. Top with remaining bread buttered side uppermost. Sprinkle with remaining sugar.
5. Beat together eggs milk and add the 2 tbsp of preserve. Pour over bread. Allow to stand for 30 minutes.
6. Cook for 12-15 minutes on DUAL COOK (on 200°C microwave MED-LOW) until the pudding is set.

450g (1 lb) shelled broad beans
225g (8oz) French beans - trimmed
2 red skinned apples, cored and cubed
1 x 15ml (1 tbsp) sesame oil
150g (5oz) natural yoghurt
1 x 15ml (1 tbsp) wholegrain mustard
1 x 15ml (1 tbsp) lemon juice
397g (14oz) can red kidney beans,
minced and drained
seasoning

Apple Bean Salad

1. Place broad beans, and french beans in a bowl, add 2 x 15ml (2 tbsp) of water, cover and cook for 9-11 minutes on HIGH until tender.
2. In a bowl mix together the oil, yoghurt, mustard, lemon juice. Add drained cooled beans, kidney beans and apple. Toss and season to taste.

50g (2oz) butter or margarine
1 medium onion - chopped
60ml (4 tbsp) plain flour
425ml (¾pt) milk
150ml (¼pt) cider
340g (12oz) can sweetcorn - drained
175g (6oz) cheddar cheese - grated
½ red pepper - seeded, cut into strips and blanched
6 x 15ml (6 tbsp) fresh brown breadcrumbs

Cheesy Corn Bake

1. Place butter or margarine and onion in a large bowl and cook for 2 minutes on HIGH to soften onion. Stir in flour.
2. Heat milk in a bowl or jug for 2 minutes on HIGH. Gradually whisk into flour mixture.
3. Microwave for 2-3 minutes on HIGH until thick. Whisk in cider and microwave for a further minute on HIGH.
4. Blanch the strips of pepper by placing in a large bowl with 2 x 15ml (2 tbsp) water, covering and microwaving for 2 minutes on HIGH. Drain.
5. Mix sweetcorn, 100g (4oz) cheese, pepper and seasoning into sauce. Turn into a microwave-proof serving dish and sprinkle with remaining cheese and breadcrumbs.
6. Microwave for 5 minutes on HIGH to heat through. Stand for 2 minutes and serve.

1 onion - peeled and chopped
1 red pepper - seeded and chopped
½ x 5ml (½ tsp) chilli powder
1 x 5ml (1 tbsp) olive oil
1 spring onion - chopped
1 x 5ml (1 tsp) paprika
1 x 5ml (1 tsp) ground cumin
1 x 5ml (1 tsp) sugar
3 x 15ml (3 tbsp) tomato purée
1 x 5ml (1 tsp) salt
¼ x 5ml (¼ tsp) tabasco sauce
175g (6oz) long grain rice
450ml (¾pt) water

Hot Stuffed Tomatoes

1. In a heat proof dish mix oil, onion, red pepper, chilli powder, paprika, spring onion, ground cumin, sugar, tomato purée salt and tabasco sauce.
2. Heat for 2-3 minutes on HIGH.
3. Add rice and 450ml (¾pt) water. Cover and cook for 15 minutes on HIGH. Stir half way through. Allow to stand for 5 minutes.
4. Slice the top off each tomato and set aside. Scoop out the centres of the tomatoes.
5. Fill each tomato with the filling and replace the top.
6. Place the tomatoes on a dish. Cook for 1-2 minutes on MED-HIGH.

Stuffed Courgettes

1. Slice courgettes in half lengthways and place them into a large dish. Cover with microwave plastic wrap and cook for 3-4 minutes on HIGH until soft.
2. Scoop out the courgette flesh, chop, and mix with remaining filling ingredients. Spoon filling into courgette skins.
3. Prepare cheese sauce. Melt margarine for 30 seconds on HIGH, stir in the flour and blend in the milk. Cook for 3-3½ minutes on HIGH until thickened.
4. Whisk the sauce until smooth and stir in the cheese, whisk until cheese is melted.
5. Pour cheese sauce over the courgettes and heat 3 minutes on HIGH until warmed through.

3 courgettes
1 x 200g (7oz) tin tomatoes - chopped
1 clove of garlic - chopped
75g (3oz) peeled prawns
salt and pepper

Cheese sauce:
25g (1oz) plain flour
25g (1oz) margarine
300ml (½pt) milk
50g (2oz) cheddar cheese

Bean Curry

1. Place all ingredients in a large casserole dish and stir together well. Cover and cook for 5 minutes on HIGH. Stir well.
2. Reduce power to MED-LOW and microwave for 65-70 minutes, stirring twice during cooking time.
3. Stand for 10 minutes and serve.

340g (¾ lb) textured soya protein in cubes
1 medium onion - chopped
1 green or red pepper - seeded and chopped
1 clove garlic - crushed
400g (14oz) can tomatoes
400g (14oz) red kidney beans - drained
60ml (4 tbsp) tomato purée
1 x 5ml (1 tsp) dark brown sugar
1½ x 5ml (1½ tsp) curry powder
seasoning to taste
300ml (½pt) vegetable stock

Pease Pudding

1. Mix drained peas with the onion, bay leaf and thyme in a large bowl. Cover with water and cover bowl with film. Cook for 5 minutes on HIGH.
2. Reduce power to MEDIUM and cook for a further 30-35 minutes.
3. Remove bay leaf and mash the peas and onion to form a soft pulp. Add egg and butter and stir to melt butter.
4. Transfer mixture to a 900g (2 lb) pudding basin. Cover and cook for 8-9 minutes on MED-HIGH.
5. Allow to stand until cool and turn out of basin. Serve hot or cold, cut into wedges.

225g (8oz) dried yellow peas - soaked overnight
25g (1oz) butter
½ small onion - quartered
1 bay leaf
pinch of thyme
½ egg - beaten
seasoning to taste

Nutty Burgers

1. Mix cheese with breadcrumbs and two thirds of the walnuts. Add onion, carrot and curry powder/paste. Season.
2. Add half of egg to bind mixture together, reserving remainder.
3. Divide mixture into 4 and form round burger shapes. Brush the burgers with remaining egg and then coat in remaining walnuts.
4. Place on heatproof dish and chill in fridge for at least 1 hour.
5. Place dish on high rack and cook for 10-11 minutes on DUAL COOK GRILL (microwave MED-LOW/GRILL) turning burgers over two thirds of the way through cooking time.

100g (4oz) finely grated cheddar cheese
100g (4oz) wholemeal breadcrumbs
100g (4oz) shelled walnuts - finely chopped
100g (4oz) onion - finely chopped
1 medium carrot - peeled and grated
1-2 x 5ml (1-2 tsp) curry paste or powder (to taste)
salt and pepper
1 egg - lightly beaten

225g (8oz) wholemeal plain flour
pinch of salt
100g (4oz) hard margarine (to grate from freezer)
4 x 15ml (4 tbsp) cold water
1 x 15ml (1 tbsp) vegetable oil
100g (4oz) carrots - sliced
100g (4oz) leeks - sliced
100g (4oz) celery - sliced
100g (4oz) cauliflower - into florets
100g (4oz) sweetcorn kernels
100g (4oz) mushrooms - thickly sliced
25g (1oz) butter
25g (1oz) plain flour
450ml (³/₄pt) milk
75g (3oz) grated strong cheese
seasoning
1 x 15ml (1 tbsp) chopped fresh parsley
425g (14.2oz) can drained red kidney beans
beaten egg for brushing

Country Vegetable Pie

1. Place wholemeal flour and salt into a bowl, grate in margarine. Mix lightly together with water and vegetable oil to form a firm dough. Do not overhandle it. Place into a plastic bag and cool.
2. Place carrots, leeks, celery, cauliflower and sweetcorn into a large casserole dish. Add 5 tablespoons of water, cover and cook for 10 minutes on HIGH.
3. Place butter in a large jug. Heat for 1 minute on HIGH. Stir in flour, heat for 30 seconds on HIGH. Blend in grated cheese.
4. Mix seasoning and chopped parsley into the sauce. Stir sauce into vegetables together with kidney beans and mushrooms. Spoon vegetables into a pie dish and place a pie funnel in the centre.
5. Roll out the pastry 2.5cm (1") larger than the pie dish. Cut a strip off to cover the rim of dish. Brush with a little egg. Roll pastry top over the filling. Trim and flute edges, using any left-over pastry for decorations.
6. Bake for 18-22 minutes on DUAL COOK (on 200°C microwave MED-LOW). Allow to stand for 5 minutes before serving.

1 cauliflower - cut into florets
225g (8oz) broad beans
225g (8oz) mange tout
175g (6oz) baby sweetcorn
2 shallots - peeled and chopped
225g (8oz) carrots - peeled and sliced
50g (2oz) nuts eg. cashew
25g (1oz) desiccated coconut

For the sauce:
25g (1oz) margarine
25g (1oz) wholemeal flour
2 x 5ml (2 tsp) curry powder
1 x 5ml (1 tsp) ground turmeric
1 x 5ml (1 tsp) ground cumin
1 x 5ml (1 tsp) garam masala
300ml (¹/₂pt) milk
2 x 15ml (2 tbsp) double cream
seasoning

Vegetable Curry

1. In a bowl place all the vegetables add 4 x 15ml (4 tbsp) water, cover and cook for 12 minutes on HIGH. Strain off water. Stir in the nuts and coconut.
2. In a bowl melt the margarine for 1 minute on HIGH. Blend in the wholemeal flour, curry powder, ground turmeric, cumin, garam masala, gradually add milk.
3. Cook for 3-4 minutes on HIGH - Stirring half way through, add the double cream and season to taste.
4. Pour the sauce over the vegetables.
5. Cover and reheat for 4-5 minutes on HIGH.

Vegetable Scone Bake

1. In a bowl place the cauliflower florets and carrots, add 2 x 15ml (2 tbsp) water. Cover and cook for 10 minutes on HIGH. Drain off water.
2. In a bowl place the leeks and celery, and 25g (1oz) of butter. Cover and cook for 8 minutes on HIGH.
3. In a bowl melt the remaining butter for 30 seconds - 1 minute on HIGH. Stir in wholewheat flour, and the vegetable stock. Cook for 2-3 minutes on HIGH, until thickened add cashews.
4. Mix all ingredients together. Season to taste.
5. For the scone mixture - in a bowl mix together the self raising flour, mustard and salt. Rub in the butter until the mixture resembles fine breadcrumbs.
6. Mix in the grated cheddar cheese. Beat the egg into the milk. Mix together with other ingredients until a smooth dough is formed.
7. Roll out on a floured work surface until 2½cm (1″) thick. Cut into rounds.
8. Pour the vegetable mixture into a heat-proof casserole dish. Place the scones towards the edge of the dish. Brush scones with milk.
9. Place on low metal rack. Cook for 16-18 minutes DUAL COOK (on 200°C microwave LOW).

½ cauliflower - cut into florets
3 carrots - peeled and chopped
4 leeks - peeled and sliced
4 celery sticks - sliced
50g (2oz) butter
25g (1oz) wholewheat flour
300ml (½pt) vegetable stock
50g (2oz) cashew nuts - roughly chopped

Scone mixture:
225g (8oz) self raising flour
½ x 5ml (½ tsp) salt
50g (2oz) butter
75g-100g (3-4oz) mature grated cheddar cheese
1 x size 3 egg - beaten
150ml (¼pt) milk
1½ x 5ml (1½ tsp) dry mustard

Barley Hot Pot

1. In a bowl place the barley and cover with double volume hot water. Cover and cook for 20 minutes on HIGH. Allow to stand for approx 40-50 minutes. Drain.
2. In a heat proof dish place the oil, onion, garlic, celery and leeks. Cook for 2 minutes on HIGH.
3. Add the courgettes, carrots and mushrooms. Pour over the stock. Add the barley, chopped parsley, tomato purée, soy sauce, seasoning to taste. Stir well. Cover and cook for 30-40 minutes DUAL COOK (on 160°C microwave LOW).

225g (8oz) pot barley soaked
1 x 15ml (1 tbsp) vegetable oil
1 large onion - peeled and chopped
3 cloves garlic - peeled and crushed
4 celery sticks- chopped
2 leeks - chopped
3 courgettes - sliced
350g (12oz) carrots - peeled and sliced
225g (8oz) button mushrooms - sliced
600ml (1pt) vegetable stock
3 x 15ml (3 tbsp) parsley chopped
1 x 15ml (1 tbsp) tomato purée seasoning
1 x 15ml (1 tbsp) soy sauce

Spicy Wild Rice

1. Place rice in a large bowl with the water. Cover and cook for 5 minutes on HIGH. Then 14-16 minutes on MEDIUM. Allow to stand for 5 minutes.
2. Place broccoli florets, red pepper, celery and spring onion into a large dish with 2 tbsp of water. Cover and cook for 3 minutes on HIGH.
3. Stir cooked drained rice into vegetables with chopped parsley, lemon juice, tabasco sauce, soy sauce, oil and seasoning. Stir well and serve.

175g (6oz) brown rice
25g (1oz) wild rice
900ml (1½pt) hot water
225g (8oz) broccoli florets
1 small red pepper - thinly sliced
1 stick celery - sliced
4 spring onions - finely chopped
2 x 15ml (2 tbsp) chopped parsley
2 x 15ml (2 tbsp) lemon juice
1 x 5ml (1 tsp) tabasco sauce
1 x 15ml (1 tbsp) soy sauce

CHILDRENS COOKERY

Chocolate Mousse

100g (4oz) plain chocolate
4 x eggs size 3 (room temperature)
separated
1 x 5ml (1 tsp) vanilla essence

1. Break up chocolate and put into a bowl, melt, uncovered for 2-3 minutes on HIGH. Allow to cool slightly.
2. Beat in egg yolks and vanilla. Beat whites stiffly and using a metal spoon fold into chocolate mixture.
3. When smooth and evenly combined transfer to 4 individual ramekin dishes or glasses. Refrigerate until firm.
4. Decorate with cream.

Pussy Cat Pizzas

75g (3oz) self raising flour
75g (3oz) wholemeal flour
1 x 5ml (1 tsp) baking powder
25g (1oz) grated cheese
1 x 5ml (1 tsp) Marmite
120ml (4fl. oz) milk

Topping:
1 x 100ml (4oz) tube tomato purée
50g (2oz) mushrooms, finely sliced
1 x 5ml (1 tsp) mixed herbs
100g (4oz) grated cheese
few kernels of corn
small piece of red pepper
few whole almonds

Witches need a pussy cat as a faithful companion. Make these easy pizzas in a pussy cat shape. Cut out the template from paper first.

1. Make the pizza shape. Draw a pussy cat (about 10cm (4")) on a piece of paper and cut it out to make the template.
2. Make the pizza dough. Mix the flours, baking powder and cheese in a bowl. Place the Marmite and 1 x 15ml (1 tbsp) of the milk in a jug. Cook for 30 seconds on HIGH to dissolve the Marmite. Stir in the rest of the milk. Mix to a soft dough with the flour.
3. Roll out on a floured board to ½cm (¼'') thick. Cut out 6 pussy cat shapes, place onto greaseproof paper.
4. Spread each with tomato purée and sprinkle lightly with herbs. Divide mushrooms evenly between them. Top with grated cheese, make eyes from corn kernels, noses from almonds and mouths from red pepper.
5. Cook for 6-7 minutes on HIGH.

Rum Truffles

225g (8oz) plain chocolate, broken into
pieces
a few drops rum essence
100g (4oz) stale cake
100g (4oz) ground almonds
50g (2oz) icing sugar
50g (2oz) chocolate vermicelli

1. Place chocolate and rum essence into a bowl and heat on HIGH until chocolate melted, 2½-3 minutes. Stir well to make a smooth mixture.
2. Crumble cake and ground almonds together in a bowl with the fingertips. Pour in the melted chocolate and icing sugar and stir well to combine.
3. Turn onto a board sprinkled with icing sugar and knead lightly until smooth.
4. Shape the mixture into aprox. 25 balls and roll each in the chocolate vermicelli. Chill in the refrigerator until firm.

Makes about 25.

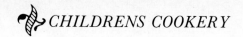

50g (2oz) butter or margarine
30 white marshmallows
150g (5oz) rice crispies
½ x 5ml (½ tsp) vanilla essence
600ml (1pt) your favourite ice cream
foil
1 cocktail stick
1 postage stamp

Igloo Pudding

What could be more amazing and impressive than building a completely edible igloo?

1. Grease and line a swiss roll tin. Put butter and marshmallows into big bowl, cook for 2 minutes on HIGH until melted.
2. Stir in rice crispies and vanilla essence.
3. Pour into the greased tin and press down evenly with your fingers.
4. Mark into squares as soon as the mixture is cool enough to handle.
5. Make a small circle of squares on a sheet of foil with two pointing outwards to form a doorway. Then build another layer on top pressing the squares together to seal the edges. When you get to the third layer, slant the squares over slightly and press, together to form the covered roof. Put two squares over the doorway to cover it.
   N.B.   You must work quickly, if the squares get too hard to shape, just pop them in the microwave for 30 seconds to soften.
6. Leave the igloo in the fridge for at least 15 minutes. Then fill the centre with ice cream. Store in the freezer until ready to serve.
7. Make the flag, lick the end of the stamp and stick it onto the cocktail stick and plant it in the roof of the igloo.

50g (2oz) butter
50g (2oz) castor sugar
grated rind of ½ lemon and
10ml (2 tsp) lemon juice
1 egg yolk
100g (4oz) plain flour
25g (1oz) icing sugar
1 tube Smarties

Traffic Light Biscuits

1. Cream together butter, castor sugar and grated lemon rind, until light and fluffy.
2. Beat in egg yolk and plain flour. Bind together with lemon juice.
3. Roll out into a square (8") square. Cut into 10 rectangles measuring 4 x 10cm (4" x 1½").
4. Place onto a greased baking sheet (25cm diam) and cook on low wire rack for 10-11 minutes CONVECTION 200°C.
5. Allow to cool on wire rack.
6. Mix icing sugar with 5ml (1 tsp) cold water and mix into a smooth paste.
7. Stick Smarties onto biscuits to make traffic lights.

100g (4oz) plain flour, sifted
½ x 5ml (½ tsp) bicarbonate of soda
2 x 5 ml (2 tsp) ground ginger
½ x 5ml (½ tsp) ground cinnamon
50g (2oz) demerara sugar
2 x 15ml (2 tbsp) golden syrup
25g (1oz) butter or margarine
1 x 5ml (1 tsp) milk

Gingerbread People

1. Mix together flour, bicarbonate of soda, ground ginger and cinnamon.
2. Place sugar, golden syrup and butter in a microwaveable bowl and heat on HIGH for 1-1½ minutes until butter is melted, Stir.
3. Mix flour mixture with melted ingredients and 5ml (1 tsp) milk, to make a firm dough.
4. Wrap in cling film and chill for 30 minutes in refrigerator.
5. Roll out onto a floured surface to a 5mm (½'') thickness. Using gingerbread cutters cut out.
6. Place tray on low wire rack and cook for 10-11 minutes on CONVECTION 200°C.
7. Allow to cool on a cooling rack.

Chocolate Hedgehogs

1. Cream margarine and sugar together until pale and fluffy, gradually beat in egg, self raising flour and milk.
2. Divide mixture into 12 well greased round bun or tart tin.
3. Cook on low wire rack for 11-13 minutes on CONVECTION 200°C until golden.
4. Remove from tin and cool on wire rack.
5. Cream together butter and icing sugar until light and fluffy. Place chocolate in a heat-proof dish and warm for 1-2 minutes on HIGH microwave until melted.
6. Stir chocolate into cream mixture with the milk until well mixed. Spread butter cream over the round side of the buns shaping to form a snout. Decorate with jelly tots, for the nose, coloured balls for the eyes halved chocolate buttons for the spikes.

50g (2oz) castor sugar
50g (2oz) soft margarine
1 egg, size 3
50g (2oz) self raising flour
1 x 15ml (1 tbsp) milk
225g (8oz) icing sugar
100g (4oz) butter
2 x 15ml (2 tbsp) milk
50g (2oz) dark chocolate
chocolate buttons, coloured sugared balls, jelly tots

Sausage Snails

These can be hot or cold. Serve them on a bed of lettuce.

1. Wrap a rasher of streaky bacon around each sausage. Place on a plastic rack. Place a mushroom in the centre of each to form a shell. Cover with crumpled kitchen paper.
2. Cook for 6-7 minutes on HIGH.
3. Meanwhile cut small sticks of carrots to be antennae. Stick two in each snail.
4. Secure the mushroom shell with a little pâté or cream cheese just before serving.

6 rashers of rindless streaky bacon
6 chipolata sausages
6 button mushrooms
1 small carrot
little cream cheese or pâté

Funny Face Toffee Apples

This is a quick way of RECYCLING ADULT SWEETS in a more artistic way. Older children could do it themselves but take care as the toffee gets VERY HOT. Great for a rainy day at half term or for a party treat. These toffee apples can be wrapped in greaseproof or plastic wrap for the party goers to take home in their goody bags!

Try it with other fruits - smaller pieces of pear, plum, banana, etc., then roll them in sesame or popy seeds, vermicelli or hundreds and thousands.

Magic Method

1. Wash and dry the apples. Push wooden skewers through the centre.
2. Place toffees and water in a large heatproof bowl.
   Cook for 2½-3 minutes on HIGH or until toffee has melted. Stir halfway through melting.
3. Twirl the apples in the toffee until coated. Stand on greaseproof paper.
4. While still warm, decorate with sweets. Use 2 smarties for eyes, almonds for nose, ¼ glacé cherries for mouth and ears, and vermicelli for hair.

Secret ingredients:
6 small eating apples
450g (1 lb) treacle or softy chewy toffees
1 x 15ml (1 tbsp) water
1 tube smarties or tiny toy jellies
4 glacé cherries
6 whole almonds
chocolate vermicelli
6 wooden skewers

INDEX